Close the Interaction Gap

Discover, harness, and accelerate the collaborative potential of your leaders, teams, and organization

Max Isaac
Anton McBurnie

Bridge Publishing

www.3circlepartners.com

Bridge Publishing
1040 N. Maple, Suite A
Marysville, OH 43040
USA

To Lorraine, Lindsay, and Heather whose love and support I appreciate so much.

—Max

With many thanks to my family. I simply wouldn't be me without you.

—Anton

Acknowledgments

If you want to learn about the necessity of interacting effectively, collaborate on a book. We have known each other more than 20 years—first as business professionals, then friends, and later business partners—and still had to close our own "interaction gaps" to create a book that reflects the blending of two aligned but distinct perspectives.

At every step of the way, we were reminded about why it's so valuable to be able to draw out the talents of others around us. For example . . .

Once again we are deeply indebted to Sue Reynard. We have worked with Sue on previous books and she has demonstrated her outstanding ability to boil ideas down to their essence and assist us in communicating them clearly. We also thank her for her infinite patience, working with the two of us, and her ability to call us to account when needed (as it frequently was!).

Maggie Carveth, Lindsay Isaac, and Meredith Roedel provided stellar support to us in handling the myriad of logistical issues that arise in writing and publishing a book, and these seem to multiply at least threefold when two people decide to collaborate as authors.

Every vignette and case study in this book is a disguised explanation of real world events. We thank the many individuals and teams we have worked with over the years for providing such a rich source of experience that enabled us to write this book. Many of the ideas in the book were honed in discussion and collaboration with our colleagues at 3Circle Partners in both Europe and North America and we greatly value and appreciate your feedback and support.

There are several individuals who willingly gave of their time to read our manuscripts during various stages of its development, including Rick Ayers, Ken Bouchard, Christine Komola, Joe Mazzulo (yes

Joe, we finally finished it), Michael Ritter, Dana Vogen, Daniel Wallace and Jeanne Young.

Many thanks to Nigel Belbin, Jo Keeler and the entire team at Belbin Associates in Cambridge, U.K. who have been a wonderful counsel to us as we have collaborated with them over the years.

Finally, we would be remiss in not mentioning Dr. Meredith Belbin as an inspiration to us all to "play to our strengths and manage our weaknesses." We thank him for being so kind as to write the Foreword to this book.

Contents

Foreword... xi

Introduction: Why Interaction Matters.. 1

How to *See* and Tackle Interaction Gaps...................................6

Part 1:
Understanding the Impact of
Interaction Gaps

Chapter 1: Closing Performance Gaps
With Improved Interaction 11

Hard Data Sheds Light on a Soft Issue................................... 12

From Stalemate to Success.. 16

Making Interaction a Priority.. 21

Chapter 2: Recognizing
Interaction Gaps.. 23

Symptoms of Interaction Problems 24

Interaction Gaps Personified: The Doomed Corporate Initiative...... 29

Where Are Your Interaction Gaps?....................................... 32

Chapter 3: Closing the Gaps 33

Case 1: Executives Lead the Way... 33

Case 2: Solaris Done Right.. 34

Case 3: Project Team Achieves Results in Record Time 36

Case 4: Leadership Team Effectiveness 37

Believing in a More Effective Future 38

Epilogue: Taking Action to Improve Interaction...................... 39

Part II

Components of Success:
The Fun, Mundane, & Tricky

Prologue: Avoiding the Fatal Flaws..................................... 43

Flaw #1: Head Over Heart—
Ignoring emotions and defensiveness 44

Flaw #2: The Tower of Babel—
Failing to create a shared language around interaction.................. 47

Flaw #3: The Gravity of Habit—
Underestimating the power of group norms 48

Flaw #4: One-and-Done—
Failing to transfer skills from theory to reality 53

Creating Your Own Approach.. 53

Chapter 4: Fun 1 – Finding the Ferraris 59

Team Role Model: A Framework for Understanding
Collaborative Strengths and Weaknesses 60

Finding YOUR Parked Ferrari: The Impact of Self-Knowledge........ 64

Improving Your Personal Impact.................................... 67

Team Improvement (The Power of Team Maps)...................... 71

The Joy of Personal and Group Effectiveness 77

Chapter 5: Mundane 1– Conquering the Meeting Beast......... 79

Start With the "Why?"... 80

Match the Who (and How Many) to the Why....................... 84

Keep It Simple and Practical....................................... 90

When the Simple Is Hard... 94

Continually Learn to Improve Your Meetings 95

Chapter 6: Mundane 2 – Walking the Talk on Alignment 99

Misalignment Creep... 101

Staying Aligned: Walking the Talk Takes More Talking..................... 106

How Aligned Are Your Teams? 108

Chapter 7: Tricky 1 – Developing a Feedback Habit.............. 109

The Barriers to Feedback 111

Step 1: Group Feedback on Group Processes........................ 113

Step 2: Interaction Feedback in a Group Setting.................... 114

Step 3: Develop 1-on-1 Feedback Skills.............................. 118

Using Disclosure To Encourage Feedback........................... 118

Learning to Love This "F" Word 122

Chapter 8: Tricky 2 – Constructive Use of Conflict.............. 125

The Bad and Ugly, and The Good....................................... 127

The Best Preventive: Trust... 130

Making Differences an Asset: The Secrets
to Constructive Conflict.. 132

How to Recover from a Blow Up 137

Getting Past Strong Conflict: Leaving the past behind............ 140

Conclusion... 142

Epilogue: From Novelty to Routine 143

1. Give People a Reason to Care...................................... 144

2. Develop a Strategy Based on Team Role Composition........ 144

3. Use a Coach in the Early Stages.................................... 145

4. Start Slow 146

Balancing the Fun, Mundane, and Tricky 148

Part III
Playing Three-Dimensional Chess

Prologue: Pulling the Pieces Together 151

**Chapter 9: Improving a Leader's "IQ"
(Interaction Quotient)** 153

Tuning In to Your Interaction Style 154

Continuous Learning 160

Increase Your Versatility 163

Promoting Better Interaction Around You 164

Improved Leadership Effectiveness 169

Chapter 10: Start with the Home Team 171

Step 1. Current State and Pain Points 172

Step 2. Individual Interaction Skills 176

Step 3. A Team Interaction Plan 176

Making It Real: Case Studies in Team Development 179

An Individual and Collective Experience 186

Chapter 11: Three Deployment Options 187

Silo Busting 188

Booster Shot 192

Cascading & Viral Models 195

Take Down the Hurdles 203

Foreword

BY

MEREDITH BELBIN

I am delighted to be asked to write a Foreword to this book. Max and I both have had global experience in helping firms to fulfill their potential and have reached similar conclusions in many areas. That is what inspires us to pass on any lessons learned.

Nonetheless Max and his co-author Anton have developed their own way of approaching the gap in communication issues at all levels. Words are important triggers for thought and action. A key word in this book is Interaction Gap. Its existence means that the failure to communicate comes at a heavy price. The resulting loss of awareness and understanding can have long-term damaging effects on an organisation.

This Interaction Gap (or the IG) brings to mind other two-letter duos in common use—IQ and EQ. This pair is being commonly used to denote some key points about individuals. IQ stands for the intelligence quotient. Generally we prefer to have intelligent rather than unintelligent members to work with. But what about EQ? This depicts emotional maturity. In differentiating the successful from the unsuccessful, experience has borne out some key lessons. Many with very high IQs disappoint in delivery. Brains are no guarantee of common sense nor do they give assurance against making political blunders. On the other hand this shortfall can be overcome by the possessors of high EQs. Of course we need the merits of both in a balanced team. These simple letters, IQ and EQ, operate as a form of shorthand for busy executives in discussing candidates for placing and appointments.

Now we can add new initials to our semantic armoury in any overview of the firm. Does it suffer from an IG problem. If so, where does it occur? Max and Anton tell us about the various levels where it can be found. We need to focus on any "lack of alignment between individuals and teams." Reducing the gap improves morale and raises business performance.

This book offers rich and abundant material. So how should it be approached? One suggestion is to search through and underline the passages you think especially telling. Different people may cite different passages as having key importance. That could be a strength. A good follow-up can then be for readers to meet and explain to each other why some points struck them above others. That formula for shared learning is one way of finding a consensual route for moving forward.

All that now remains for me to say is—good reading and don't forget to use what you have learned.

Meredith Belbin
Cambridge, England

Why Interaction Matters

For years, two key product development teams in the R&D department of a well-known business equipment manufacturer had managed to turn out successful products despite having strong differences in how they approached their work. One team—engineers who specialized in new technology—was regarded by the other team as process geeks. They were very analytical, created map after map of the workflow, and were obsessed with measurable, duplicable improvements. The other team, which had end-to-end process responsibility, was regarded by the process geeks as being cowboys: undisciplined, willing to try anything to see if it worked, making decisions on the fly.

While relations between the teams were tense, they managed to get work done by dividing it up along strictly functional lines. The workarounds they put in place to avoid having to deal with each other weren't efficient but enabled them to get their work done more or less on schedule. That division of labor seemed to be fine ...

... until the company upped the stakes by challenging the teams to scale up a technology used in a consumer device for enterprise-level demands and requirements. The CEO felt that using the existing technology in a brand new way was essential to push the envelope and help preserve the company's market leadership.

Suddenly, these teams found themselves in a high-pressure, high-profile situation, needing to work closely together to achieve a functional design for a breakthrough product with an aggressive launch date.

It didn't take long for the veneer of civility to fall away under these conditions. The teams simply could not reach decisions. Their meetings dragged on, they got very little done, and each side pointed fingers at the other to explain the lack of progress. The cowboys were discouraged because every time they brought up a new idea, the other side "would want to run 50 tests." The process geeks were equally frustrated: "Those guys are all opinions and no data. They keep coming up with solutions that no one can duplicate!"

The project leaders, recognizing the breakdown of communication between the two teams and unsure what to do, first tried focusing them on the product development process. They defined steps. They talked about goals and priorities. Neither action helped. They tried talking about the importance of collaboration and emphasized that everybody really needed "to get along." No go. They even asked the Senior VP in charge of the effort for help, but he told them, "Just go fix this. I shouldn't need to get involved."

So the stalemate continued—and the product release date kept getting pushed back further and further until it looked like the official product launch would be at least a year late.

This lack of progress frustrated the senior leadership. Many teams fail when they aren't clear on their priorities, lack management support, involve the wrong people, and so on. But none of those factors were the case here. In fact, the company had done a lot right:

- There was a clear sense of urgency around the product development effort. Everyone in the company knew how important it was for this project to be a success. Leaders were keenly aware that every day of delay meant a substantial amount of lost revenue.

- There was strong management support. Senior managers were very much behind the project and willing to provide the team with any resources it needed.

- The team members were some of the best and brightest in the company, experts in their respective areas. Collectively, the areas of expertise needed to create a breakthrough product were all represented on the team.

- The company had embraced process improvement principles long ago and knew how to run successful projects.

If you look at this list, you'll see everything they did fell into the two traditional dimensions of organizational effectiveness: strategy and execution. Yet that was not enough. There had to be something else standing in the way of progress (Figure 1).

Figure 1: What's Missing?

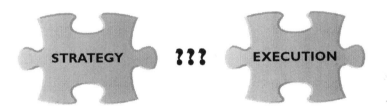

What was missing was mastery over a third critical dimension of organizational effectiveness: what happens when people try to deal with one another to get work done. That covers everything from whether people can exchange ideas or not, whether someone trusts someone else, and who plays what role in decision making, to what people say and how they say it, who gets listened to and who doesn't, and who gets assigned which tasks. And that's just the tip of the iceberg. This human dimension to organizational effectiveness is what we call interaction (Figure 2).

Figure 2: Three Dimensions of Effectiveness

By definition, interaction concerns situations where human beings are dealing with one another, either 1-on-1 or in some configuration that involves groups, teams, departments, or even entire organizations. The nature of interaction is influenced by many factors, including everything from company policies around collaboration to personality differences. Sometimes the combination of factors leads to common understanding, insight, and action. At other times, it leads to conflict, division, and stalemate.

These kinds of interaction issues are too often labeled dismissively as "soft stuff," problems too intangible to manage and therefore unworthy of serious attention. But in our experience, every company has undiagnosed problems with interaction that negatively affect their bottom line to a greater or lesser degree. Poor interaction not only leads to stalemates like our product development teams encountered but also bad decisions, untapped talent, and turf wars. It harms creativity, productivity, efficiency, and even civility—all of which compromise trust, respect, and morale.

These problems lead to shortfalls between what people and groups hope to achieve and what they actually achieve. These shortfalls are what we call **interaction gaps**. They happen because people are unable to pool their talents, perspectives, knowledge, and collaborative skills effectively. Interaction gaps come in all shapes and sizes, imposing costs both great and small.

Large interaction gaps can impede or even destroy key strategic initiatives, such as the product development teams we were just discussing. There's more on that story in Chapter 1. Another example of a large interaction gap that we discuss in the book is based on the experiences of a senior executive in charge of a major strategic initiative who did not see any significant value in collaboration. He thought it was enough that he brought his direct reports together once a month to provide updates on progress. He discouraged any direct communication between the project teams, believing it to be an unnecessary distraction from getting on with their "real" work. Though the program had captured a lot of low-hanging fruit early on, as time passed the initiative became marginalized and the organization began seeing very little return on the thousands of hours and sizeable dollars invested in the initiative. (See p. 29 for more on this story.)

On the smaller end of the scale, interaction gaps limit the effectiveness of individuals and teams. A very accomplished sales rep, for example, was promoted and placed in charge of a sales division. He struggled to fit the mold of what he thought a leader should be, and took on tasks that he was ill suited for, such as running meetings, trying to coordinate the team's activities, and so on. He didn't know how to best utilize the collaborative talents of his team. Soon, his team had the worst performance in the company.

Here is another example: Data on participation in an 11-person management team showed that 6 of the managers barely spoke up at all in the team's regular meetings. Best case? Their participation wasn't needed, so the regular meetings *merely* represented a waste of their time. That's bad enough. But the worst case is that they had information that would have helped the team better understand the matter at hand and likely make better decisions, but were afraid or reluctant to speak for whatever reason. The cost of making decisions based on incomplete information may be unknowable but is no less real than hard dollar costs. (See p. 85 for more on this story.)

This management team example hits a chord with many people. Everyone has been on teams that were dysfunctional in some way. Perhaps they participated in meetings where one or two people took up all the airtime—because the boss or team leader did not draw out the quieter members of the team. Perhaps someone on the team thought they had all the answers, a participant simply liked the sound of their own voice, or the wrong people were in the room to effectively deal with the issue at hand. No matter the reason, in all of these cases an interaction gap was created that prevented the group from performing at its full capability.

Surely you have run into these kinds of situations in your own work experience, or perhaps other examples of people or groups who couldn't use their human capital effectively. If so, then you will benefit from learning how to master effective interaction, which is the subject of this book.

How to See and Tackle Interaction Gaps

Interaction is such a fundamental factor in how well organizations can function that, in one sense, it's surprising to us that achieving more effective interaction ("closing interaction gaps," in our terms) is so rarely made a priority. Yet, in other ways, it's not surprising at all because many leaders are taught to pay attention to strategy and execution—identifying the big goals for their group or organization and then implementing the processes and systems to get there. The need to think about the effectiveness of interaction simply hasn't been part of the picture.

Organizations that ignore the interaction dimension of organizational effectiveness are missing a vital piece of the puzzle, and their potential to work faster, smarter, and better will remain locked behind layers of poor communication, compromised decisions, turf wars, and dysfunctional group dynamics.

Unfortunately, since few managers or employees are aware of the importance of interaction, it's difficult to convince them that poor interaction might be the root cause of their problem. **Making interaction a management and leadership priority is one of the reasons we wrote this book.** We draw on more than 40 years of combined experience to help you understand what good and bad interaction looks like, and offer practical steps you can take to improve interaction in your own sphere of influence. The book is divided into three parts:

Part I: **Understanding the Impact of Interaction Gaps** goes into much more detail about what interaction gaps are, what they look like in action, and their impact on an organization. It also describes the many benefits that accrue from developing a clear understanding and mastery of interaction.

Part II: **Components of Success—The Fun, Mundane, and Tricky** describes the three streams of activity you need to work on to create sustainable improvements in interaction. Some of the up-front work is fun in the sense that people get insights about themselves and their teams. But there are also mundane (yet vital) aspects to establishing and maintaining healthier interaction patterns. And because real people with real emotions are involved in interaction, you have to be prepared to navigate some tricky waters.

Part III: **Three Dimensional Chess—You, Your Team, Your Organization** discusses specific actions that will improve your own interaction skills as well as those of your team or work group, plus how to approach the task of improving interaction on a broader scale.

Part 1

Understanding the Impact of Interaction Gaps

— I —

Closing Performance Gaps With Improved Interaction

Imagine a first-of-its-kind track event pitting the world-record-holder of the men's 400-meter hurdles against the world-record-holder of the men's 400-meter sprint. They settle into their starting blocks, then launch at full speed when the starting pistol goes off. As soon as the hurdler goes over the first hurdle, you realize he has already lost even though the race has barely begun. From then on, no matter how smoothly he clears the hurdles, the sprinter just keeps pulling away.

If we could manipulate time and bring the current world-record-holding athletes together in this fictional race, Michael Johnson would have just finished his sprint in 43.18 seconds, a good 3.6 seconds faster than—and a very obvious 33 meters (~100 feet) ahead of—hurdler Kevin Young.

Anyone who watches Olympic sports knows that a gap of 3.6 seconds, while barely noticeable in the everyday world, could make the difference between winning a gold medal and finishing last. No matter how good the hurdler is, whether it's Kevin Young or anyone else, they can't fully compensate for the hurdles that slow them down, even if they are a world-class competitor.

There are factors at work in the business world that act like hurdles on a track, serving no apparent purpose other than to slow you down and create performance gaps. One of the least recognized but most common of these factors is ineffective interaction: the inability of people and groups to work together to resolve a problem, make a decision, design a product, or simply perform their everyday work. Poor interaction limits what groups and teams can achieve, and we have been able to show this with data.

Hard Data Sheds Light on a Soft Issue

If you've ever tried to get hard, incontrovertible data on any kind of soft issue, you'll understand the dilemma we've faced over the years. How do you measure "interaction effectiveness" in a way that people can see for themselves that poor interaction has a business cost?

So that you can appreciate the nature of the data we'll be presenting, here's a brief overview of our methodology: Our approach revolves around a simulation that is presented to groups as a simple decision-making exercise. We like using a decision-making scenario because it hits on multiple dimensions of interaction that occur all the time in real life, including everything from if and how people share ideas with others to how authority or seniority are used.

During the decision-making exercise, we ask teams of participants to analyze a management situation and come up with answers to 20 questions. Each individual answers the questions first on their own, then their teams discuss the questions and have to agree on a final "team answer" for each question. We then calculate the scores and look at three sets of numbers:

1) Individual scores based on individual answers

2) Team scores based on the agreed-on team answers

3) The **best possible score** each team could have achieved

To get the last number—the best possible score—we go through each question where the team answer was incorrect and ask if any *individual* on the team had the right answer. If at least one person had the correct answer to that question, we award those points to the team. (The best possible score therefore represents information that was available to the team if only they knew how to tap into it.)

You can see a typical example of "actual team scores" vs. "best possible scores" in Figure 3, which represents data from the last dozen times we ran this simulation (we have not weeded out any bad teams or good teams).

Figure 3: Measuring the Interaction Gap

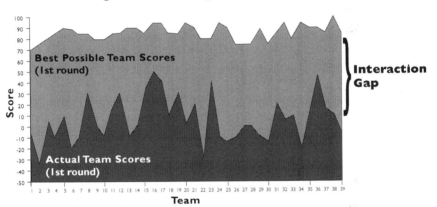

Every participant gets the same information to review and is asked to answer a set of 20 questions on their own. Then the teams discuss the questions and come up with a team answer for each of the 20 questions. To score the results, we add the points for all the correct answers and subtract points for each incorrect answer—just as in life, there is a penalty for being wrong. In theory, an individual or a team can score anywhere from +100 points (all answers correct) to −100 points (all answers wrong).

It's not hard to pick out the pattern on the chart. The actual team scores range from about -40 to +50 points (negative scores are possible because we subtract points for incorrect answers). By comparison, the average best possible team score is 85 points. So even the *best* teams are scoring 35 points below their potential, and most are 80 to 100 points below what is possible. (The same is true for the individuals on the team, as discussed in the sidebar.)

This measurable difference between the *potential* achievement of the group and the *actual* achievement level is the best way we've found to quantify interaction gaps.

Interaction Gaps = Untapped potential

The patterns in Figure 1 and Figure 2 have held true for thousands of teams, no matter their composition (managers, executives, frontline staff in the office or on the factory floor) or purpose (functional or project teams, product development groups, ongoing department work groups, ad hoc committees, or problem-solving teams).

The message is loud and clear: **Every single team has the knowledge and resources to make better decisions than it actually does at first.**

 After pointing out that fact, we get our groups to think about *why*. They are all given clear goals, information, and processes, but fail to achieve the potential represented by the "best possible scores." What is going on that limits their achievements initially?

The answer is **poor interaction**: the people on the team, alone and collectively, don't know how to share their knowledge, skills, and ideas in ways that could enable their *group* to outperform all of the *individuals*.

Throughout the rest of the simulation, we teach people some key concepts and skills (covered later in this book). Gradually they realize that they can get the highest possible scores only if they get better at tapping into the knowledge of *all* the team members. Figure 5 (on page 16) shows the results they get by the last round of the simulation we

Smart individuals aren't as smart as teams

When some people see the data in Figure 3, they protest: "Not so fast. Surely there are some bright people on the team who have much higher individual scores but the team as a whole decided on a different answer! This is proof that the group just drags them down." (That's the argument that more than a few "smart" people have given us as the reason why they don't like to collaborate on anything; they think they can *always* do better on their own.)

If you're one of these skeptics, Figure 4 is for you. We've taken the team data from Figure 3 and imposed the best *individual* score from each team. It's the white line in the graph below.

Figure 4: Overlaying the Best INDIVIDUAL Scores

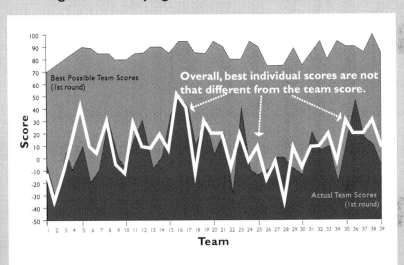

What can we conclude? Yes, individuals can collectively outscore their team about half of the time, although not by much. However the potential represented by the team is always greater than that of any single individual, even if the team is made up of the company's best and brightest.

This data clearly shows that collaboration is not just desirable but *necessary* to maximize team results, especially when dealing with complex issues.

were just describing, overlaid on the actual scores of the first round and the best possible score from the first round.

Figure 5: Narrowing the Interaction Gap

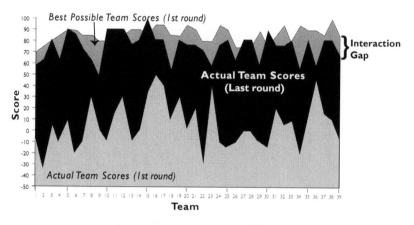

Average improvement was 68 points.

As you can see, once people know how to deal with each other more effectively, the teams regularly score in the 70–90 point range. Some teams even outscore their "best possible score" from the first round. All the sample teams—no exceptions!—achieve much better outcomes with much smaller performance gaps than when they started.

But what's far more important than the results of a single simulation is what happens back on the job. To discuss that, let's return to the product development teams featured in the introduction.

From Stalemate to Success

You might recall that two teams needed to collaborate to develop a challenging new product. One team was geeky engineers known for their rigor; the other team was the shoot-from-the-hip cowboys who were creative and impulsive. The "super team" was trapped in a stalemate that caused the launch of a new product to get pushed back again and again. Traditional interventions such as discussing the team's goals and purpose and encouraging everyone to get along did nothing to move the team forward. That's when the company turned to us for help.

By the time we came on the scene, it was clear that the two groups had developed unproductive patterns of interaction. They blamed each other for problems and were unable or unwilling to find value in the other side's approach or ideas. Each side had withdrawn into its silo, posting a Keep Out sign prominently.

To break them out of this pattern, we ran the decision-making simulation just described using mixed groups (half cowboys, half geeks). Over the course of the simulation, these groups—like all the other groups that go through the scenario—realized they got the best results when they worked together and used all of the knowledge, talents, and perspectives of everyone in their group. They couldn't follow *just* the geek or cowboy instincts. Combining their knowledge and perspectives was the fastest way for them to get the right answers.

As a result of this experience, the product development teams became aware that the way they had interacted in the past—the assumptions present when they discussed issues, the way they framed problems, what they said to each other and how they said it—was holding them back. That gave them the incentive to do something about this unrecognized dimension of effectiveness.

In a follow-up session, we put the combined teams through what is known as a mirroring activity. Each side documented their perceptions of themselves and of the other side, then the two teams came together to share and discuss their perceptions. They didn't use the labels cowboys and geeks like we have here, but the underlying message associated with those terms was clearly communicated for the first time. In discussing their own team's and the other team's perceptions, the participants come to a better understanding of the other side in the conflict. The mirroring activity doesn't actually resolve conflicts or decide who is right or wrong, but it does allow the groups to move past their conflicts into constructive problem solving. (If you are unfamiliar with this technique, you can find a more detailed description on page 140.)

Together, the mirroring activity and decision-making simulation helped both sides start to think differently about each other, acknowledge that there was a huge interaction gap, and begin to recognize the ingredients that would lead to more effective interaction. Attitudes started changing fundamentally:

- The more conservative, process-oriented geeks originally saw only the rash and reckless side of the cowboys. Ultimately, they came to also appreciate the cowboys' energy and creativity. They realized that the innovative thinking brought by the cowboy group was needed to solve the technology challenges they were dealing with. In other words, the creative action-orientation of the cowboys was no longer seen as a problem or weakness; it was one of the skills needed for a high-performance team.

- Similarly, the more fast-acting cowboys at first saw only that the process geeks took a very long time to make decisions, mostly because they spent "forever" analyzing data and were very reluctant to consider novel ideas. The cowboys came to realize that the analytical skills, discipline, and rigor of the geeks could lead to products that were more reliable and easier to use and produce. That ability to apply critical thinking skills came to be seen as another one of the talents needed for team success.

In short, each side realized that they would have a very hard time developing a successful new product if they relied only on their own skills and perspectives. In other words, they *needed* their differences to solve the challenges.

These changes in attitude opened the door for improved interaction. For one thing, the two sides actually began truly interacting. Instead of avoiding each other, sniping whenever they did get together, and blaming each other for the failure to make progress, they began talking about the issues that divided them.

Problems weren't solved overnight. After all, the interaction issues had been brewing for years. However, the door had been pried open. The only question remaining was whether they would choose to walk through the door or retreat to their previous positions.

The first test came in a later meeting where we had the combined group identify the issues they argued over the most and those where both sides had to agree in order to move forward. Altogether, they identified more than a dozen issues they needed to resolve. We then began the slow process of working through these issues one by one.

To give you a sense of how these discussions worked, here's an example: One of the hottest areas of disagreement was around goal alignment. Both sides agreed on the overarching goal of delivering an innovative new product with satisfactory quality, but they disagreed on the definition of what that meant. The geek side argued for sticking close to established quality standards because they knew the company had the capability to meet current standards. The cowboy side wanted to set new and higher standards for the competitive advantage it would bring, even though it wasn't clear how much effort it would take to do so. Despite these strong differences, they were able to reach decisions on a definition that would meet the high standards of their customers but still allow them to meet the business need to finish the development of the new product.

Over the next few months, the team worked on the rest of the issues, all of which were eventually resolved. There were still a number of heated discussions but the team now had the tolerance and incentive to look for the positive aspects between divergent opinions. **They were able to do what high-performing groups do:**

- They listened respectfully to what the other side had to say on a subject and gave each idea careful consideration rather than dismissing it out of hand. Everyone was interested in discussing the merits and limitations of each perspective, and they began looking for ways to *combine* insights and approaches into creative solutions rather than battle over who was right.

- They learned how to discuss interaction issues and challenges—tone of voice, dismissive statements, assumptions, etc.—in ways that didn't raise hackles.

- They learned how to assign tasks and responsibilities to the people best suited to the work.

And there you have the core of effective interaction—appreciating the necessity of working together. The realization of this necessity brought better awareness of talents, contributions, and weaknesses, thereby helping people close the gap between what they wanted to achieve and what they were able to achieve.

By applying these interaction skills to the product design effort, the product development teams were able to achieve their goal within months. The company also reported that the launch of this product was one of the smoothest in its history and the product had a record-low number of post-launch problems.

In a post-launch interview, a leader of the product development project commented that the knowledge and skills the teams now possessed to face and resolve issues themselves very quickly made a huge difference in speeding up the development of the critical new product. They had learned to recognize emerging or potential interaction gaps and knew what to do to resolve the issues before the gap became insurmountable.

Effective interaction doesn't mean you will never run into interaction problems. It means you will have the skills and willingness to *work through* tough issues rather than let them stop you in your tracks.

Making Interaction a Priority

When we first talk to executives about interaction challenges in their organization, it's not unusual for their eyes to glaze over. They're thinking that we're going to talk about the psychology of why "Diane and Sanford don't get along" or something similar. But that's not our focus at all. The fact that Diane and Sanford don't get along or don't seem to be able to agree on anything may be irrelevant to the company—and if so, it's irrelevant to us.

What we're interested in are interaction problems that harm the business in some way. We're interested in interaction gaps that lead to underutilized potential and wasted time and resources; gaps that represent unnecessary costs both hard and soft. For example, what if Diane is the head of R&D and Sanford is the head of marketing and their conflict is making it harder for the company to bring new products to market? That kind of interaction gap is clearly relevant and could cost an organization significant lost revenue.

Working to reduce interaction gaps has an impact on every single person in your organization. Just think about what it takes for you (and everyone else in your organization) to do your work every day. We know that the majority of your work involves interaction: connecting with other people to reach decisions, coordinating work, generating ideas, analyzing a problem . . . the list goes on and on.

In fact, we've started asking executives to tell us how much of their time is spent working alone vs. interacting in some way (one-on-one, one-on-some, or with a full team or group). The answers are shown in Figure 6. As you can see, the executives we've surveyed spend on average about 25% of their time working alone; the other 75% involves some form of interaction.

Figure 6: Interaction Time of Executives

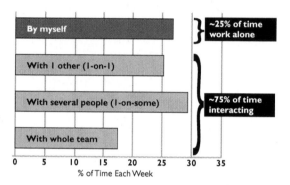

Even if your percentages are skewed more towards solo work, we're still betting that you spend a substantial amount of time each week needing to work with and through other people. Now think about the impact it could have on your overall effectiveness if you could use your interaction time more effectively, no matter if it's just 10% of your time, 90%, or somewhere in between. Learning how to improve interaction can have as big an impact on a leader's overall success as how well they develop viable strategies and/or manage execution.

Though we haven't formally surveyed a wider range of employees, we see the same general trend organization-wide: a significant amount of almost every employee's time involves interaction. Who wouldn't want to make sure they were using that time most effectively?

The starting point in reducing interaction gaps is learning to recognize poor interaction, as we'll talk about in the next chapter.

—2—

Recognizing Interaction Gaps

A company whose last president had left unexpectedly brought in a new president, James, from the outside. It soon became clear to James that there was a lot of what he would label as "craziness" going on that no one inside the company seemed to notice. Members of his executive team were quick to blame each other for problems. There was a complete lack of innovation anywhere in the company. Staff would get different answers about business priorities depending on which executive they talked to.

One particular problem that caught James' attention was the animosity between Ken (head of engineering) and Derek (head of production). The two of them didn't get along at all, and the attitudes cascaded down through their departments. The production group saw themselves as "customers" of the engineers and would try to boss them around; the engineers didn't respond well to that treatment and would drag their heels when responding to calls for help. It got so bad that it wasn't unusual for the production line to be stopped for a full day or even two while the problems were sorted out. Ken and Derek would send flaming emails back-and-forth—copying the rest of the executive team, of course. Crazy.

As an outsider, James could see these problems quite clearly. But to insiders, it was just business as usual. Or perhaps a better phrase would be "non-business as usual."

Most of us have been in situations where our perspective as an outsider allowed us to see "crazy" in something that the participants saw as business as usual (even if acknowledging it was annoying and frustrating). True, sometimes these situations where people and groups seem to be working against each other rather than toward a common goal can be traced to poor strategies or ineffective business practices. But more often than not the problem is rooted in how people interact with each other.

What does an interaction gap look like? Learning to recognize interaction gaps is a critical first step that creates the motivation to look for solutions to help close those gaps. For that reason, this chapter talks about what interaction gaps look like and the impact they have on organizational effectiveness.

Symptoms of Interaction Problems

Let's be clear, you have interaction problems in your company. Some of them—such as turf wars or silo conflicts between groups that don't get along—are easily identified as "bad interaction." But many interaction problems get labeled as something else because people don't see that poor interaction is the root cause. For example:

- A strategic initiative fails. Was it because the strategy was incorrect—or was it because the group charged with implementation couldn't resolve their differences of opinion?

- Six months after the fact, your leadership team realizes it made a poor executive decision. Was it an honest error in judgment— or was the decision made by the people with the loudest voices rather than the people who had relevant information?

- A company suspects there is widespread duplication of effort. Is it from poor planning—or maybe no one at the executive level gave department or functional heads a chance to discuss their responsibilities, identify overlaps, and sort out who will do what?

When you're trying to identify interaction problems in your own organization, here are some of the more common symptoms you see that indicate an underlying problem with interaction.

People in constant conflict or experiencing culture clashes

Part of the product development stalemate was due in large part to culture clashes: the geeks and cowboys had very different ways of thinking about and dealing with issues. This kind of fundamental difference in mindset is common when people come from different specialties or departments that favor different skill sets (HR vs. finance, for example). It is also very apparent after mergers and acquisitions where the companies have different cultures.

Conflict in these situations is common because people have unstated assumptions—they assume that everyone is looking at a problem or issue with the same perspective, which is why they can't understand how other people could come to completely different conclusions. Since these assumptions and perspectives are never identified, however, they are never challenged and the conflict continues.

Groups or individuals can also be in conflict for a variety of other reasons. Perhaps they have ongoing disagreements about priorities or goals, or who has the final decision. We hear story after story from leaders who are constantly being dragged in to referee arguments that their staff "should be able to solve on their own."

The worst-case scenario with ongoing conflict is what we call **death by silo**: the groups or organizations expend so much energy dealing with arguments and dysfunction that their real work is neglected. They limp along, perhaps managing to get their work done by employing workarounds. But any task that requires input or real cooperation from other groups is a painful chore.

Unexplained team failures or struggles

We routinely ask groups, "Over the last 12 months, how many of you have been on a truly high-performance team?" At best, 5% to 10% of the people raise their hands; all of them describe their experiences as very fulfilling and enjoyable. When we start exploring why this figure is so low—why so many teams are *not* high performing—the people we're talking to often blame the usual suspects: no clear purpose, management support was lacking, "too many teams, not enough time," project scope creep, or constantly changing team membership.

But we also hear many stories where the source of trouble was more of a mystery. People say that one of their teams "seemed to be firing on only a few cylinders." Or they will describe symptoms like "the team did good work but it took us forever to reach the milestones that we set for the project" or "we couldn't seem to get beyond data analysis" or "we achieved the goal, but it was so painful!"

Oftentimes, these kinds of vague problems can be traced to poor interaction. Teams will have a hard time completing their work if, for example, they assign collaborative responsibilities to the wrong people. Ever been on a team where someone who was a habitually poor organizer was in charge of coordinating tasks? Or one where the quietest and most introverted member of the team is charged with developing external relationships? Or the least collaborative person is in charge of running meetings and making decisions?

The stories throughout this book illustrate many other types of interaction problems. Maybe some of those examples will sound familiar and help explain some mysteriously failed teams in your own past.

Compliance without commitment

Almost every businessperson we know has been involved in a change initiative that eventually died away because the people involved in making the change happen only *complied* with the decision. They were never really committed to it, never took ownership of the implementation, and simply went through the motions while doing their best to avoid responsibility or accountability.

With few exceptions, this compliance-without-commitment problem can be traced to the way in which the people instigating the change interacted with those who were expected to implement the change. The "interaction" was probably top down—orders coming from the drivers to the implementers—which typically happens in three situations:

1) The manager does not value collaborative interaction, the "I decide, they go execute" mentality.

2) The manager has tried more-collaborative approaches in the past only to see things go haywire as teams get mired in endless cycles of discussion and indecision—which brings the manager to conclude that the only way to make progress is to make the decisions unilaterally.

3) The manager thinks the matter is urgent and doesn't have the time to get input up front (a phenomenon very typical in fire-fighting-type cultures).

While there are certainly situations where unilateral decision making is appropriate and necessary, that is seldom the case when the decision requires those implementing it to make significant changes and to sustain a level of commitment over the long haul. In those situations, true interaction—the exchange of ideas, perceptions, and insights—is needed to come up with a plan that will be supported by all.

Stifled contributions

People at all levels—frontline to executive suite—tell us about times they've wanted to speak up in meetings to present important information or views, but kept silent because they didn't want to get shut down or get caught in a fruitless debate. Decisions were then made based on what the people with the loudest voices, most seniority, or the most (perceived) expertise said. Other members of the group did not contribute in any meaningful way, even though they had excellent ideas or valuable input.

We also hear from many employees who tell us they think they would resolve problems faster if they could collaborate with colleagues in other departments, but are discouraged from doing so. Inter-department or even cross-team collaboration has somehow become taboo. In some cases, they may have already been told by their manager to "work as a team" or "be collaborative," but when they try to work with others, the manager's reaction is, "What the heck are you doing? Trying to work with those guys will just slow us down or derail us!" (That kind of mixed messaging is demoralizing.)

In these situations, effective interaction is shut down completely, and the interaction gaps just keep getting larger.

Avoidance of participative approaches

A major company with a well-known brand name went through a series of presidents who did not see the value in having the senior executives work together in any meaningful fashion. The company's executive team now consists of six managers who operate as independent silos. There are no turf wars because there is no contested territory—each executive has a kingdom that they run however they want.

Does this qualify as an "interaction gap" even though these managers aren't interacting? Most definitely! The company is paying a severe penalty for its non-collaboration. While individual departments may be run effectively, a closer look exposes huge waste and duplication because these senior managers do not really work *with* each other. They do not share ideas or resources. As an example, the company has separate and almost identical training programs in multiple departments.

While this story illustrates non-collaboration at a corporate level, the same phenomenon occurs in many other guises. There is the manager who uses the hub-and-spoke method of only having 1-on-1 meetings with their direct reports. There is the supervisor who has given up on collaborative decision making because it seems to take too long.

Interaction gaps that are created because people are avoiding participative approaches are very hard to recognize because there is no outright conflict. What you do see, however, is a group or team or department that never quite lives up to its synergistic potential.

Interaction Gaps Personified: The Doomed Corporate Initiative

About a decade ago, a major global corporation decided to launch a new strategic program that we'll call the "Solaris Initiative." The new CEO was convinced that Solaris was a critical element in the company's strategy. He strongly supported the initiative and, employing a collaborative approach, gained the full support of senior and mid-level executives. The initiative was successfully launched with a lot of fanfare and a massive training effort began.

A very seasoned senior VP who had been with the company for years—we'll call him Adam—was put in charge of Solaris, even though he had no prior experience working on anything like Solaris. Every manager with direct Solaris responsibilities reported to Adam, who then reported to the CEO.

The Solaris Initiative did provide the business results the company was looking for at first. But while people respected Adam and agreed that he was a smart guy, he was one of those managers who was very uncomfortable with the human side of business. He didn't see much value in collaboration, and preferred keeping power and knowledge to himself. As a result, the Solaris leadership meetings were perfunctory, with each manager simply reporting out what was happening in their area. There was little discussion, sharing of lessons learned, or collaborative problem solving.

That's why support for Solaris eventually waned and everything began to deteriorate. Adam's direct reports even tried holding meetings on the side (without him) so they could talk through common challenges, but the workaround became too difficult to manage and they eventually gave it up. The problems with the Solaris Initiative didn't stop there:

- Adam approved the purchase of various computer support systems that he thought would facilitate the use of the Solaris processes in the company, but he didn't consult with others or consider the user friendliness of the systems. They are still in place today, but they are more of a drag on Solaris than a help. Still, since the technology represents a significant cost in both time and money, management is hesitant to scrap the investment and find a better solution.

- Adam did such a good job of implementing a clearly defined hub-and-spoke system that the various spokes soon lost track of what the others were doing. As a result, not long into the effort there was a massive duplication of Solaris effort among the various fiefdoms.

The Solaris Initiative in this company was soon gasping its last breaths. Within a few years, there was very little executive interest and the effort became completely marginalized.

If anything in business qualifies as crazy, this waste of resources surely does! This organization invested millions of dollars in training, had devoted thousands of hours of staff time to this initiative, all for very little payback after the initial stages in which the low-hanging fruit opportunities were exploited. (Sound familiar?)

That's why we consider Adam a prime example of the huge impact that failure in the interaction dimension can have when it happens at the senior levels. He was placed in the leadership position so he could help the company execute a vital new strategy. He had all the technical knowledge he needed, but as he freely admitted, "I don't do touchy feely." He simply didn't pay attention to if and how well people were collaborating. He wasn't really interested in whether people felt free to exchange ideas or kept their creativity locked inside themselves. Because he didn't pay attention to these issues, he was never able to fully utilize the considerable talents of his direct reports. Plus, he made the situation worse by implementing practices that *prevented* collaboration between the departments involved in Solaris.

Above all, Adam failed to recognize the negative impact that his behavior had on the people around him and on the effectiveness of the Solaris Initiative. His behavior contributed to big interaction gaps that doomed the Solaris Initiative to becoming just another very expensive program-of-the-month. And in case anyone underestimates the incredible drain this is on company resources, the generally accepted figure from researchers is that around 70% of corporate initiatives like Solaris fail!

Where Are Your Interaction Gaps?

Well? Did you recognize yourself, people you know, your team, or a prior work experience in any of the examples of poor interaction described in this chapter? We rarely run into someone who hasn't had at least one of the problems we covered. And for the rare few who haven't experienced these specific issues, we hope you're starting to realize that interaction matters and that the interaction gaps come in many shapes and sizes.

A gap can be a problem between one individual and another. Perhaps there is a difference in style or approach that leads people to mistrust or misinterpret each other. Or the gap can be the failure of groups to connect or understand each other effectively, resulting in big problems for their teams, departments, and organization.

What we also hope you'll start doing is thinking about the ways in which ineffective interaction could contribute to problems you see in your own workplace. Poor interaction often represents a major barrier that impedes results, whether in major initiatives or everyday productivity. Poor interaction is like many toxins: imperceptible and localized at first, but if allowed to accumulate, capable of destroying the effectiveness of an entire system—and that system could be your company.

Imagine you were an outsider coming into your organization, like the newly hired CEO described at the beginning of this chapter. He saw behaviors that didn't make sense for the business but that employees took as "just the way things are." What would you see as an outsider that you might label as "crazy" in your current organization?

Once you become attuned to observing interaction gaps, you'll start noticing the many ways in which poor interaction is holding back performance in your organization. With that awareness, you'll also start to think about the benefits that can be gained from closing those interaction gaps. We'll give some examples in the next chapter.

Closing the Gaps

What you can expect from improved interaction

Just as the negative effects of interaction gaps appear in many shapes and sizes, so too do the benefits. If your situation is like the product development team in Chapter 1 that was able to stop the delays and release a new product, you might be able to put a hard dollar figure on your gains. But more often, the benefits accrue in terms that are harder to measure, such as shorter meetings (something everyone appreciates), improved decision making, and greater utilization of team resources. Below are four examples to illustrate these points.

Case 1: Executives Lead the Way

This is the "after" story of James and his executive team that we introduced at the start of Chapter 2. James was an outsider brought in as the new CEO of a high tech company. Much of what he observed at first appeared "crazy" to him. Two of his direct reports, Ken and Derek, seemed to be at loggerheads and their inability to work together trickled down into their departments.

When the executive team was first exposed to the concept of interaction effectiveness and interaction gaps, Ken and Derek realized just how much they were contributing to the problems in the lower ranks. Derek was an impatient, command-and-control type of person and would simply give people directives if they came to him with issues. Ken was a patient, participative problem-solver. People who came to him for advice were likely to end up in a long discussion of the pros and cons of different approaches. Their different communication styles also led to many unintended problems: Ken and Derek often *thought* they were in complete agreement on an overall direction after their meetings, but different perspectives would start to evolve once they were on their own. Since they both thought (erroneously) they had started from a common viewpoint, they each blamed the other when things fell apart. Their inability to work together led to competition rather than cooperation between their departments.

Becoming aware of these problems was just the first step. Ken and Derek worked together over a period of several months to become clearer about goals and responsibilities. What surprised them both was that neither had to change their management style. Rather, they got better at identifying up front when Ken's participative style was a better choice and when Derek's more direct approach was more appropriate. They also worked to become more consistent in messaging, which had a positive trickle down effect among the rank and file. Basic operations improved almost immediately and over the next year their two departments exhibited much more innovation in problem solving. At every level, meetings are now 20–30% shorter and groups no longer duplicate work done in other groups.

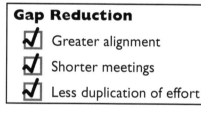

Gap Reduction
- ☑ Greater alignment
- ☑ Shorter meetings
- ☑ Less duplication of effort

Case 2: Solaris Done Right

A major corporation was implementing something similar to the Solaris Initiative described in Chapter 2 (which ended up not

> ## Managing differences, not eliminating them
>
> One of the most surprising lessons when it comes to closing interaction gaps is that people do not have to try to change who they are. As Ken and Derek discovered, they could collaborate quite effectively once they learned to take advantage of the different strengths each of them brought to the table and to soften the impact of their weaknesses (Derek could be a bit abrasive at times and Ken sometimes overemphasized broad consensus). They came to see their differences as assets rather than roadblocks and were able to help each other manage their weaknesses. We'll talk more about this concept in Chapters 4 and 8.

delivering anywhere near its full potential). From a technical standpoint, this second company did everything the Solaris company did: they appointed a senior executive to oversee the effort, established a network of project leaders and teams, and implemented a widespread training program to provide new technical skills.

In addition to these standard elements of any major deployment, this company also established a plan for incorporating and practicing interaction skills. They did not want interaction gaps to get in the way of executing their plans, so they built a foundation around:

- Making sure their plans included commitments and actions related to collaboration, teamwork, decision making, and so on.

- Training anyone who was leading any piece of the initiative on interaction fundamentals. Leaders knew what they had to do to create an open environment where all issues—ideas, criticisms, input, insights—could be discussed freely.

- Investing in identifying people's collaborative skills and talents.

- Setting up mechanisms for communication between groups that needed to work closely together if the initiative was to succeed.

- Establishing a process of frequent checking for alignment so that all the groups could be sure they were still working towards common goals.

As a result of paying attention to their interaction effectiveness, the Solaris-like effort in this company started on a strong footing and is still flourishing years later because it continues to deliver significant business results. In terms of enriching the culture of this organization, the management methods promoted by the initiative have achieved broad acceptance and are now part of the organization's norms and DNA.

> **Gap Reduction**
> Investment produced major gains
> ☑ Greater participation
> ☑ Swift adoption of new concepts

Case 3: Project Team Achieves Results in Record Time

Thomas was a project leader at a large international company where management identified long cycle times on projects as a major area for improvement. It was not unusual for projects to take 12 to 18 months to complete.

At his request, Thomas's teams went through training on interaction in addition to regular project skills training. The cycle time on his projects dropped to between 4 and 5 months.

When asked what made the difference, Thomas said that the skills he and his team had gained in interaction had been the most significant success factor in his team's performance. For example, they had made the effort to identify and capitalize on the mix of collaborative skills present on their team. They used that knowledge to improve every aspect of the team's interactions: how they discussed issues, made decisions, coordinated their efforts, sought out help, invented new solutions, and so on.

Thomas cites an example of where a major gain in meeting effectiveness was achieved when one team realized that only two of its six members really loved doing the data analysis. To make sure the whole team avoided "paralysis by analysis," Thomas set up separate meetings where the two analyzers could slice and dice the data to their hearts' content. The analysis fiends then reported their findings to the full team. In this way, the team was able to gain from these people's thorough analysis without slowing down its progress.

Being smart about how he used the talents on his team cut out wasted time and energy and built a reputation for Thomas's teams as the fastest and most effective in the company.

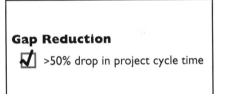

Gap Reduction

☑ >50% drop in project cycle time

Case 4: Leadership Team Effectiveness

A senior management team at a medium-sized tech manufacturing company hated their periodic leadership meetings. The leader of this team, a senior vice president, was clever and creative, a real visionary, and also something of an absent-minded professor. However, he thought that part of his job was to keep the team organized, so he'd call meetings but wouldn't tell people what the meeting was about, he would send out prep work to only some of the attendees, and sometimes he would even forget to invite key people! So much time was wasted at the beginning of every meeting just getting organized that the team struggled to make even the simplest decisions. One of the managers was so frustrated with the lack of action that he even became aggressive on occasion.

As we described with the product development groups, a key part of the solution for this team centered around getting team members to recognize and appreciate the collaborative strengths and weaknesses on the team. **They learned how to benefit from the differences rather than chafe at them**. For example, the team needed to find ways to benefit from the executive's creativity but not be held back by his disorganization. So the organizing and follow-through responsibilities were shifted to someone who was very good at that kind of work. Similarly, the team recognized that the super-frustrated manager had a good point about the lack of decision making and action, and they made him the timekeeper so that he could call a halt to discussions and move the team along whenever appropriate.

By being aware of their collaborative strengths and weakness, the team was able to exploit the former and make the latter irrelevant in terms of overall effectiveness. Once these interaction issues were straightened out, meetings were shorter and more productive, and became enjoyable.

> **Gap Reduction**
> ☑ Shorter, more productive meetings
> ☑ Improved decision making

Believing in a More Effective Future

The single biggest barrier to improved interaction is the sense most people have that the conflict, frustration, or non-collaboration they are experiencing can't get better. They accept dysfunction as just the way things are. The examples in this chapter and spread throughout the book demonstrate that poor interaction doesn't have to be accepted. Without a vision of a better future, there is no motivation to improve. What we hope to do with this book is create a vision of a more effective future with significantly smaller interaction gaps.

Taking Action to Improve Interaction

T he more that organizations learn to recognize the impact of poor interaction, the more they understand that improving interaction should be a priority. They also realize that they've been giving it short shrift in the past.

"We have a dot problem," said an executive in a strategy session we were facilitating for a high tech company. We had asked their leadership team how much time and effort they'd put into refining the strategic direction for the company, how much they'd focused on operational (execution) issues, and whether they'd paid attention to their human capital by addressing interaction. We had them draw three circles on a flipchart to represent the answers they'd given, with the size of each circle reflecting the relative investment of energy in that area over the past year (Figure 7).

The executive team agreed that their main focus the prior year had been in the execution circle. However, they felt they had put the appropriate amount of effort in the strategy circle, with a lesser, but still adequate, effort in the interaction circle.

Figure 7: Executives' perception of emphasis

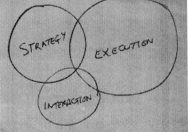

During a break in the strategy session, we had the opportunity to ask a group of directors and managers who reported to the leadership team how they would draw the same three circles based on their view of where the leadership team spent its time and energy. The result is shown in Figure 8.

As the executives from this company were looking at the alternative diagram, we asked them another question: "Do you have a strategic plan for your company?" They said, "Yes." So we asked, "Do you have an operational plan to execute that strategy?" They said, "Yes."

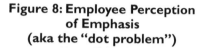

Figure 8: Employee Perception of Emphasis (aka the "dot problem")

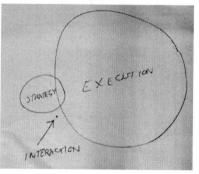

Finally, we asked, "Do you have an interaction plan for your company?" They pointed at the dot and said, "No." That's when one executive commented, "We have a dot problem. It's clear we haven't put enough attention on interaction." He then added, " . . . and isn't it the interaction circle that really slows us down?"

Many of the companies we deal with have a similar "dot problem." They haven't put much effort into thinking about interaction or identifying ways to improve it. The rest of this book is focused on how to solve dot problems. Part II discusses three types of fundamental elements that should be included in any solution. Part III describes the three basic levels of intervention you should consider: 1) working on yourself as an individual, 2) working with your group or team, and 3) creating an organizational shift towards improved interaction.

Part II

Components of Success:

The Fun, Mundane, & Tricky

Avoiding the Fatal Flaws

The new CEO of a Fortune 200 company was much more of a consensus builder than his autocratic predecessor. He could see that the culture wasn't very supportive of his style, but firmly believed that better discussions and alignment at the top were critical for the company's continued growth. He brought in a well-respected consulting firm that touted its "formula for high performance cultures." After an initial flurry of activity, their prescriptive approach was abandoned as being unworkable.

#

The executive team of a consumer products company recognized that the marketplace was changing faster than the company could adapt. They decided to turn to their internal training & development department to help them launch a strategic initiative to improve collaboration and innovation. The training department did a great job of developing new courses on topics such as brainstorming techniques, meeting management, and communication skills. Six months down the road, nothing had really changed.

#

A company involved in a major Lean Six Sigma implementation learned from team leaders that many teams were struggling—having a hard time getting organized, completing commitments, delivering results. The teams had all received training on the technical skills of process improvement, so the company decided it was time to invest in "soft side" training. The HR department offered all team members the chance to undergo a range of the usual personality tests. Afterwards, the teams got together, discussed the results, and had interesting discussions about issues like extroverts vs. introverts. Yet months later, nothing had changed at either an individual or team level.

These examples illustrate just a few of the ways in which companies, teams, and work groups attempt to address poor interaction. These types of interventions for improving collaboration or solving interaction issues can sometimes have a beneficial effect on morale in the short run but seldom lead to lasting changes in interaction because they suffer from four fatal flaws that we like to describe as:

1) **Head Over Heart:** Ignoring the impact of emotions and defensiveness

2) **Tower of Babel:** Failing to create a shared language around interaction

3) **The Gravity of Habit:** Underestimating the power of group norms

4) **One-and-Done:** Failing to transfer skills from theory to reality

We'll review each of these flaws and describe how they hamper efforts to improve interaction.

Flaw #1: Head Over Heart— Ignoring emotions and defensiveness

In every human interaction there is an emotional aspect—what people are feeling, attitudes based on past experience that are shaping their perceptions, etc. Unfortunately, most interventions aimed at solving interaction problems either take a purely logical, instructional approach (teaching skills or techniques) or they are at best superficially emotional (such as off-site team building activities that make people feel good for a short time).

In real life, we know that emotions play a big part in many interactions. Arguments that start out on a logical note can, for example, get sideswiped by anger. People can react negatively to something based on what's going on in their personal lives, not the immediate business issue at hand. Past histories of poor interaction between groups can breed resentments that are difficult to overcome. Even positive emotions can get in the way of effective interaction. People or groups who like and respect each other may hesitate to speak up about problems or share their ideas for fear of offending the other party and upsetting the relationship.

One of the most pervasive of the emotional interaction barriers is defensiveness. In any situation where we suspect we are being attacked (whether real or perceived) our natural instinct is to protect our position, to defend ourselves. The strength of this defensive reaction varies widely from person to person and from group to group. Sometimes, it's a mild reaction—a passing thought—and the person or group stays open to hearing what the other side has to say so the reaction does not hinder interaction. But strong defensive reactions shut down communication.

Despite the omnipresence of emotions, however, most training programs on teamwork or collaboration are structured in a way that suggests logic and reason will always win the day. That's not true when emotions like defensiveness come into play. In fact, learning to recognize and deal with the emotional side of interaction is critical to success.

This isn't easy. Defensiveness in particular is tricky to deal with because it . . .

- **Is a normal protective mechanism.** That protectiveness sometimes arises out of a desire to preserve what has worked in the past. Imagine you're one of the cowboy members of the product development team we described back in Chapter 1. Before you were brought into this team, you worked with like-minded people and managed to pull off some great successes with your innovative approaches and quick action. Now you're expected to work with the geeks who think of you as reckless and impulsive because you want to act quickly. How would you react if you were a cowboy plopped into a geek team (or vice versa)? The natural reaction is to defend your position. Your style of working has created success in the past, so the problem must be with the other people—those buttoned-down engineers who, in your opinion, suffer paralysis by analysis.

- **Has many contributing factors.** Defensiveness has many sources, some related to the issue at hand (if people think someone is attacking their integrity or judgment, for example) but some are tied to other events or stresses happening in a person's life (people under emotional strain can be more defensive than usual). It's not easy to tell from the reaction what the underlying cause is.

- **Takes many different forms.** People who are defensive can either become combative (getting bristly, bossy, or controlling) or have the opposite reaction by turning inward and disengaging from the situation (becoming quiet, withdrawing). At the extreme ends, you may get people who become aggressive; others shut down entirely or act out through passive-aggressive behavior.

- **Is easier to see in other people than in ourselves.** Defensiveness is an emotional response to something, and in the middle of it we are overtaken by the emotion and unable to recognize the impact we are having.

- **Defensiveness is its own worst enemy.** If someone is told they are being defensive, the most common reaction is, "No I'm not!" Defensiveness is a primal reaction to a real or perceived threat and often creates a strong emotional response. We become protective of our own positions and unable to listen to the input we are receiving. We shut down, which prevents us from gaining any new knowledge that could help resolve the issue that caused the defensiveness in the first place. The odds of any individual rectifying their own defensive behavior are practically nil. It takes input from others, which of course defensive people aren't open to.

You can't ignore the reality that emotions are an integral part of interaction and can sometimes get in the way. The following chapters talk about strategies for reducing the odds that strong emotions or defensiveness will get in the way of effective interaction.

Flaw #2: The Tower of Babel— Failing to create a shared language around interaction

Think back on the last time you changed companies or even changed jobs within the same company. What were your first few meetings like? Odds are high there were terms, acronyms, and jargon thrown around that you didn't quite understand at that time. There is a natural tendency for organizations and groups to develop what is effectively their own language that enables them to communicate quickly and effectively. (Some of these "languages" even become institutionalized across industries or sectors, such as Lean or Six Sigma in manufacturing or Agile in software development.)

Unfortunately, most organizations lack a common language in the one place they need it the most—in the arena of interaction and behavior. So you ask your team, "How are we getting along?" and the answer is "Fine." You ask staff what impact a temperamental boss's behavior is having, and they either say nothing or make rude comments ("He's a real _____ [choose an epithet]"). In neither case do you get information that helps you understand what needs to change and how to change it.

From what we've observed, most discussions about interaction are best compared to thinking about how well the United Nations would work if all the interpreters suddenly went on strike: no one would understand the subtleties of the concepts and how to communicate them in a way that increases the chances of the ideas being understood. An absence of any agreed-upon language to represent interaction ideals and concepts leaves you with few options other than to use meaning-less words or disparaging language, which will serve only to provoke a defensive reaction (the consequences of which we discussed under Flaw #1: Ignoring emotions and defensiveness).

An important purpose of this part of the book is to present key concepts associated with interaction and the language used to discuss interaction goals and challenges so you can start building a common vocabulary with others interested in improving interaction. If your organization already has its own language around interaction, the key is to gain a shared, group-wide understanding of the concepts and a high degree of fluency in whichever language you have chosen.

Flaw #3: The Gravity of Habit—
Underestimating the power of group norms

As part of a corporate executive development program for high potential managers, Shelley was sent on a week-long leadership course at a very prestigious institute. Participating with a small diverse group of people from other Fortune 500 corporations, she went through a battery of psychometric assessments, team simulations, and seminars on leadership, decision making, managing conflict, etc. She came away with a comprehensive action plan for herself and her team.

Full of enthusiasm, Shelley returned to her team and tried to apply what she had learned. It was tough going. On her second day back she called a team meeting to present highlights from the course and her 90-day plan. She was dismayed by the decidedly lukewarm response. For example, her suggestions on how the team could improve the quality of its decisions got a mixed reaction: Several people didn't think there was a problem with how the team was handling decisions, and didn't see a need to change. Others were interested, but didn't understand enough about the different decision-making modes that Shelley talked about to find her suggestions useful.

Although she persevered and struggled on, after several weeks she acknowledged that she had made only limited progress in her personal development goals and had seen little shift in her team's performance. As she described it to us, "I found the course really excellent, but it was difficult to apply the learning in real life with all the day-to-day pressures and little support from anyone else on the team."

In our work with diverse organizations across the globe, it's become clear that, ironically, the majority of companies are looking for *individual* solutions to *interaction* problems. They want to send a few people to a workshop or provide a leader with training. If conflict is an issue, they identify one or two individuals they think are a problem and do one-on-one feedback sessions.

But interaction only occurs *between* people or groups—so any effort to improve interaction needs to include all the "interact-ees." As creative leadership expert Martin Rutte once said, "You have to do it by yourself, but you can't do it alone." To improve interaction, each individual has to change ("you have to do it by yourself") but will only be successful if they are supported by other individuals who are also changing ("can't do it alone").

This need to focus on the group or team is well known to anyone who has studied group psychology: one of the most powerful forces shaping group behavior is **group norms**, the unwritten rules about behavior and attitudes that people in a group adhere to almost subconsciously. The impact of norms on behavior is so huge that they are often called the "strong, silent hand" driving an organization.

Group norms cast a pull of gravity that is hard to escape. There is enormous, though usually unstated, pressure for everyone within a group to conform to its norms. (See sidebar.) Non-conformity means you get marginalized or kicked out of the group.

In fact, it's next to impossible to change a group's behavior if only one person, even if it is the group leader, wants to change or knows how to change. So even if you put one person through training on interaction, it's likely they will backslide if you put them back in an environment with the old norms. In fact, if you've ever tried to replace an old habit with a new one, you'll know how easy it is to slip back into the old way of doing things. To understand how difficult it is to change group norms, magnify that "slip back" effect geometrically by the number of people in the group!

Ignoring how difficult it is to change existing group norms is just one side of the fatal flaw coin. The other side of this coin is failing to take advantage of the power of the group to drive *new* behaviors when the majority of the group decides to change. That is, any impact you have on people at an individual level is magnified in size and speed when a group of people goes through the same experiences and collectively agrees to change. Providing new insights and tools to a group of people who are all willing to try new things will turbocharge the changes.

> ### How do norms develop?
>
> Psychologists and other researchers have been studying group behavior for decades. If you'd like to know more about the underpinnings of norms, how they develop and how they can be changed, the topics you should research are **convergence** (how diverse behavior becomes more similar in groups), **conformity** (the need for most people to behave like others in a group so they can belong), and **cohesion** (forces that help keep a group together). These three phenomena provide powerful forces that establish and maintain group norms even if no overt actions are taken. (We cover these topics in our previous book, *The Third Circle*.)
>
> The forces of convergence, conformity, and cohesion are totally predictable. If the group is conforming around norms that work *against* effective interaction, that will slow you down. But the reverse is also true: if the group converges on norms that *improve* interaction, the benefits will multiply quickly.

Norms can be an asset if they support better interaction or they can be an insurmountable barrier if they stand in the way. Here are examples of each:

- A **supportive norm**: In companies with good interaction, there is often a norm where people and groups stop to check their interaction processes frequently. Whether it's co-workers chatting about a business issue or a formal department meeting, someone asks the question: "Is what we're doing working? Are we getting what we need to move forward?" If the interaction is working, the group can continue. If not, it gives them a chance to self-correct and prevent wasted time. For example:

  > An expert who was providing background information at a meeting of his work group was using language and talking about ideas that the other attendees didn't understand. He was the one who asked the "Is this working?" question and when the others said they couldn't follow his explanations, he changed tactics. Instead of lecturing, he took the group out onto the factory floor to demonstrate the ideas he was trying to explain. People could easily visualize the concept, and

had much more insightful questions and ideas to contribute to the discussion. Instead of wasting an hour of everyone's time listening to what was an incomprehensible lecture, this group spent 30 very productive minutes that got them closer to their goal. That is effective interaction.

- A **barrier norm:** We often encounter groups where only a few people speak up during meetings; the others barely say a word. These groups generally don't label this pattern as "unbalanced participation," but that's what it is. And the group tacitly accepts the imbalance as just the way things are. The why of this pattern doesn't matter at the moment. Maybe the non-speakers are just naturally quiet or have been shut down in the past when they offered ideas, or maybe the group leader is so focused on moving the meeting forward that they stifle conversation. The important point is that this kind of norm makes it impossible for groups to make sure that all data, ideas, and opinions relevant to a topic are surfaced. In our experience, the people who don't speak up are almost always keeping useful information to themselves. Hidden information leads to poor, uninformed decisions. So a group with this kind of norm is putting an artificial limit on what it can achieve through the interaction of the people in the group.

One of the goals of this section of the book is to provide information and examples that will convince you to take the power of norms very seriously. Once you begin to pay attention, you'll begin to recognize the difference between norms that create a barrier to interaction and those that foster better collaboration. Then you can work to replace those norms that are unsupportive and create and emphasize more supportive norms.

Flaw #4: One-and-Done—
Failing to transfer skills from theory to reality

A very seasoned HR manager once said to us: "I typically get a call from a leader asking for a team-building event at an upcoming offsite, and could we do it in half a day or less. As I explore why they want to do this, I inevitably discover that there are some fundamental problems in the team dynamics that have often been going on for a long time. Yet somehow they believe a four-hour team-building event will fix that problem. It's very frustrating!"

Because there is an emotional component to interaction that is often ignored (Flaw #1), and because improvement requires a change in group norms not just teaching new information (Flaw #3), there are no overnight miracles when it comes to interaction. Providing new skills is part of the picture, but you will not get improved interaction from a one-and-done training event. Providing training without reinforcement serves only to reduce your credibility.

Interaction problems do not arise overnight and will not be solved overnight. They need to be treated the same way you would approach developing any capability—be it playing a sport, using a computer, or running a production line. It takes a systemic, process-driven approach so that you are not only imparting knowledge through training but also reinforcing and sustaining the changes in behavior long afterwards.

Creating Your Own Approach

Ways to address the four fatal flaws—defensiveness and emotions, a lack of shared language, groups vs. individuals, and skill- or norm-building vs. event-based training—are woven throughout the recommended actions covered in the following chapters. The chapters are grouped into three categories: the fun stuff, the mundane stuff, and the tricky stuff.

The Fun Stuff

The fun part of improving interaction involves techniques that help people learn about themselves. Here's an example:

> When a successful CFO decided to start her own company, she felt that her strengths lay in her analytical skills and the ability to finish everything she started. But a few years after her company was up and running, she had an analysis done of how employees and colleagues evaluated her ability to collaborate and work with others. The results revealed that they didn't think much of her analytical skills, but they perceived two strengths she was unaware of: she was really good at orchestrating the group (coordinating team and group activities through the assignment of tasks, keeping focused on goals, and so on) and she was much more creative than she gave herself credit for. Having greater awareness of her true talents has allowed this CFO to leverage her strengths and help make her new company more successful.

One of the biggest surprises for people is that, just like this former CFO, most of us have hidden talents that could help us interact much more effectively as individuals and in our groups. Imagine you're driving an old clunker around every day only to realize that there is a Ferrari in your garage you could be driving instead. Admittedly, part of the learning experience operates in the reverse—people realize that an interaction skill they thought was a Ferrari is in fact a car that *should* be kept in the garage!

People enjoy this aspect of building interaction skills because they are learning about themselves. They develop a much more accurate self-perception about their interaction strengths and weaknesses, as well as the things they do that are helpful or harmful to interaction. That not only helps them become more effective in any form of collaboration, but also provides a basis for professional growth.

This fun stuff is covered in the following chapter:

Fun 1 – Finding Your Ferraris. People can collaborate and interact much more effectively if they understand their collaborative strengths and weaknesses. This chapter describes a particular model that we prefer for understanding collaborative skills because of the practical insights it offers. (Chapter 4)

The Mundane Stuff

In the approach we use when helping groups and companies close interaction gaps, the fun stuff comes first. It seems to be a universal law that people love learning something new about themselves. The popularity of quizzes in magazines and on-line tests on many topics attest to this fact.

People have some fun learning about themselves and return to their everyday jobs filled with enthusiasm. They then look around and think to themselves "What next?" Just as with any new routine, there are many practical (and boring) details that you have to pay attention to if you want to create more effective patterns of interaction.

Routine things are often conceptually simple but very challenging to implement because they are seldom fun. Two important concepts for overcoming this challenge are covered in the following chapters:

Mundane 1 – Conquering the Meeting Beast. In most companies, meetings are viewed with resignation if not dread. But meetings are one of the most important venues for interaction, and the way meetings are run can greatly hinder or improve interaction. So it's a beast that must be conquered. (Chapter 5)

Mundane 2 – Walking the Alignment Talk. People underestimate how much work it takes to *get* aligned and how much more work it takes to *stay* aligned. This work isn't fun or glamorous, but finding ways to confirm and maintain true alignment is critical for effective interaction. (Chapter 6)

The Tricky Stuff

Nothing involving human behavior is straightforward, and interaction is no exception. There are a number of aspects that are tricky because there aren't any simple answers or techniques. We will focus on two tricky issues that can most easily send groups astray:

> **Tricky 1 – As Others See Us.** This chapter focuses on that often-dreaded word "feedback." All of us as human beings have an inaccurate perception of how our behavior affects others. Learning the basics of interaction feedback can help open the window for new insights in how we can become more effective. But it has to be approached with caution since feedback can easily go wrong. (Chapter 7)

> **Tricky 2 – Constructive Use of Conflict.** As the CEO in a company we work with said, "We can disagree without being disagreeable." In high-performance groups, people share their ideas even if they strongly disagree with each other. But you don't want disagreements to escalate to the point where they interfere with the effectiveness of your interaction. Finding the right balance between constructive and unconstructive conflict can be tricky. (Chapter 8)

Epilogue: From Novelty to Habit

The three components—the fun stuff, the mundane stuff, and the tricky stuff—will help you establish a foundation for good interaction no matter what your situation. You will need all three; you can't ignore any element. Without the fun stuff, people have little motivation to change and are less likely to understand the benefits of improving interaction. Without the mundane stuff, the everyday drag of inefficiencies and misalignments can poison other efforts to improve interaction. And if you don't learn to master the tricky stuff, you will never be able to get your groups past the hard times and difficult issues that we know every group eventually experiences.

The last chapter in this part of the book focuses on how to turn the fun, mundane, and tricky ideas into habits. In many ways, interaction effectiveness could be considered a performance art or sport: it takes repetitive practice and drills to build muscle memory so that doing the right things comes naturally. This chapter discusses the kinds of changes needed to replace old ways of interaction. At times, that can feel like trying to change a leopard's spots. But with persistence and consistent reinforcement it is possible to significantly improve interaction effectiveness.

Fun I – Finding the Ferraris

Improving competence and confidence in interaction

Intuitively, we all know that some people are better at some kinds of work than others. No matter how formal or informal the group, there is a shared knowledge about which specific tasks some people are better at than others. Need someone to be persuasive with clients? Then outgoing Lois is the best choice. Just don't ask her to analyze data because her eyes will glaze over. Need someone to organize a quarterly retreat? Fred should do that because he's great at detail and follow up. But perhaps he's not the best person to facilitate a meeting.

This kind of knowledge about the strengths and weaknesses of individuals is one of the hallmarks of highly effective groups. There are two hurdles you have to overcome, however: First, it can take months or years, and many interactions, to develop this awareness organically. Second, people's self-perceptions are often wrong. We all tend to undervalue work we are good at because it comes naturally and easily to us (more on this later in the chapter). Plus, we almost all will have tasks we *think* we are good at but really aren't. In short, we can't just rely on self-evaluations to find ways to optimize interaction. (There is a solid body of research that backs up this conclusion.[1])

---

1   see David Dunning, *Self-Insight: Roadblocks and Detours on the Path to Knowing Thyself* (NY: Psychology Press, 2005)

For many years we were looking for a methodology that would help individuals and groups overcome these hurdles. We wanted a framework that would help them learn much more quickly what kinds of interaction tasks people were good at (and not so good at) and allow them to get a more realistic view of their strengths and weaknesses. The approach we found that fitted this bill perfectly is a model based on Team Role theory.[2]

As you'll see in this chapter, the Team Role model is a comprehensive, practical approach to identifying people's collaborative strengths and weak points. Working through the model is essentially a process of self-discovery: individuals and groups come away with insights about their true talents and skills and a better understanding of how they can best contribute to any kind of collaborative work. That's why people find this kind of interaction work fun—after all, who doesn't enjoy a chance to learn something about themselves and how to become more effective?

In this chapter, we'll first describe the Team Role model then look at how it helps both individuals and groups learn how to play to their collaborative strengths and manage their weaknesses.

Team Role Model:
A Framework for Understanding Collaborative Strengths and Weaknesses

Have you ever wondered why certain teams run smoothly and others just limp along? Three decades ago, British social scientist R. Meredith Belbin wondered precisely the same thing. He wanted to understand

---

2   In the spirit of full disclosure: After using the Team Role model for several years and finding it very effective, we developed a relationship with the organization founded by its developer. So now our company, 3Circle Partners, is the approved distributor of these products in North America.

what attributes or aptitudes—and particularly, what combination of attributes and aptitudes—increased the odds of having a team that performed very well. Was it intelligence? A team-oriented mentality? A drive to produce results?

To answer these questions, Dr. Belbin performed a number of experiments where he analyzed the composition of teams using standard practices (individual test scores on personality, intelligence, and other tests, for example), and then measured the results from these teams. That allowed him to see if there was a relationship between the attributes or aptitudes and results.

What was unique about his work was that it didn't deal with functional propensities *("Is Sam best suited to be a welder or an accountant?")* but specifically about what it takes for a team to operate at peak efficiency. He got to a point where he could predict the success or failure of a team with surprising accuracy. One set of results (representative of several experiments) is shown in Figure 9.

Figure 9: Predicting Team Success

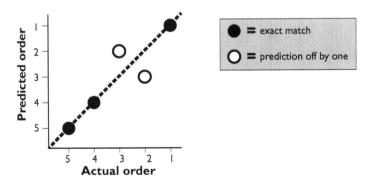

In this trial, Belbin predicted the finishing sequence of five teams by analyzing each member's aptitudes. Symbols that fall on the diagonal line represent exact matches between Belbin's prediction and the team's actual performance. The open circles show predictions that were off—but only by one rank (one team was predicted to finish 3rd but actually finished 2nd, and vice versa). Belbin had no influence on the membership of these teams.

Belbin's predictions came after he discovered that the difference between management teams that consistently achieved success and those that fell short of expectations depended on how well the teams performed in three specific skill areas:

- **Thinking abilities:** skills that help a team logically evaluate a situation (including creative and analytic skills, for example)

- **Action abilities:** skills needed for a team to get anything done (ranging from planning and organizing to pushing the group to take action)

- **People abilities:** skills that help a team work collaboratively both within the team and with the rest of their organization (such as staying connected with each other and coordinating tasks)

Belbin's work went much further. Within each of these categories, he identified three distinct Team Roles (for a total of nine roles), each of which represents a particular type of contribution to team effectiveness.

For the sake of completeness, we've included a description of the nine Team Roles in Table A. You don't need to memorize the roles, but take a moment to skim the table and we bet you'll find yourself saying, "That sounds like me," for some of these roles. You will likely recognize attributes of your colleagues or co-workers, too. (You may also find this table a useful reference in the future.)

As you can see in the table, every Team Role has two components: the special contributions that a role brings to a team and the allowable weaknesses that may get in the way of teamwork. The special contributions are the talents and skills the role contributes to a collaborative effort. The allowable weaknesses are the flipside of the special contributions—the price you have to pay to get the benefit.

Table A: Team Roles

Skill Area	Team Role	Special Contributions	Allowable Weaknesses
Thinking	Plant	Very creative; comes up with lots of ideas (some good, some bad)	Ignores anything they see as irrelevant. Can get preoccupied.
Thinking	Monitor Evaluator	Good at critical thinking; evaluating ideas; sifting through data	May slow things down.
Thinking	Specialist	Provides specialized knowledge	Contributes only in a specific area.
Action	Shaper	Hard driving; overcomes obstacles	Prone to provocation and may offend others.
Action	Implementer	Turning ideas into practical actions	Can be inflexible.
Action	Completer-Finisher	Pays attention to the details of getting everything done right	Reluctant to delegate.
People	Coordinator	Wants to get everyone on board when making decisions	Can be seen as manipulative. Their actions might be interpreted as off-loading their personal tasks to others.
People	Team Worker	Very sensitive to underlying emotions and moods	May be indecisive in crunch situations.
People	Resource Investigator	Outgoing. Enjoys making connections with others	Over-optimistic. Easily loses interest.

The allowable weaknesses are a unique contribution of Belbin's research. He showed that the very skills and traits that help someone contribute in a particular role might also make them vulnerable to some interaction problems. What makes some people good at the creative Plant role also gives them a tendency to get single-minded and ignore issues that may be important to others. (The somewhat odd descriptor

"Plant" was chosen because Belbin found in the early stages of his research that if he "planted" a highly creative person on teams, those teams consistently outperformed other teams.)

The key issue in terms of learning to deal with Team Roles is that you cannot separate the strengths (special contributions) from the weaknesses. More specifically, you often can't take advantage of the strengths unless you are willing to accept or manage the weaknesses. In fact, if you attempt to correct a weakness, you run the risk of degrading the strength. For example, look at the description of the Completer-Finisher role in the table. People who are strong in this role have a natural tendency to make sure every task is finished—and often want to do the work themselves to make sure it gets done correctly. Having someone like this on a team helps the group make sure all details of the work are completed correctly. But someone who is strong on Completer-Finisher tasks can come across as controlling because of their reluctance to delegate. Trying to force someone like this to delegate their tasks may place them under stress because it goes against their nature to let go of what other people might think of as minor details.

That said, calling a weakness "allowable" doesn't mean it can be ignored or treated as a Get-Out-of-Jail-Free card! An allowable weakness can quickly become dis-allowable if it is not managed, which we'll talk about later in this chapter.

Finding YOUR Parked Ferraris: The Impact of Self-Knowledge

Before we get into the uses of the Team Role model, it will help if you understand just a little about how the methodology works. To start the process, a person does a self-assessment on behaviors and talents associated with the roles, and then asks up to six colleagues or co-workers to evaluate them as well. The assessments by other people are critical because all of us have blinders about some aspects of our behavior when working with others. We cannot get an accurate assessment of ourselves unless we ask others to give us input.

Once the self-assessment and assessments by others are complete, all the information is combined and the person gets a set of Team Role reports that shows their relative strengths in all the nine roles and provides other analyses. The reports are rather detailed, so we won't go into them here.[3]

However, in general what you can expect to see is usually a three-way split: people will rate very highly in some roles (their **most-preferred** roles), rate low in other roles (their **least-preferred** roles), and be somewhere in the middle on the rest (their **manageable** roles). The distribution of preferred roles varies greatly. Some people have strength in all three categories (Thinking, Action, People); others will be heavily weighted in just one or two. Occasionally, we see no pattern at all—the person gets medium ratings across the board, meaning they have no obvious strengths or weaknesses (or at least are not aware of them).

When people analyze their individual Team Role information and review how they are rated on all the nine roles, four things happen almost invariably:

1) **They gain the vocabulary to talk about interaction talents and challenges.** Imagine you're an English speaker trying to teach someone who only speaks Urdu how to do your job: hard to do since you won't have a common vocabulary. That's what interaction is like in most organizations; people don't have the words to discuss interaction goals or challenges in a way that makes sense to everyone. Having the Team Roles nomenclature gives groups a shorthand system that conveys a lot of meaning.

---

3   You can find an annotated Team Role report at
    www2.3circlepartners.com/interaction-gap-resources

2) **They feel relieved and even liberated that some of their weaknesses are "allowable."** For most of their professional lives, people may have been chided to change something that other people perceived as a fault. Once they understand that strengths and weaknesses are a combination package, they realize that it's useless to try to be perfect. Instead of trying to eliminate the weaknesses, they can be more effective by learning how to manage the consequences of those weaknesses, as we'll discuss later in this chapter.

3) **They discover a Ferrari (or two) parked in their garage.** As mentioned before, most of us are blind to some aspect of the impact of our interaction style—aspects that are clear to others around us. As part of that phenomenon, the people around us will often rate us higher in some skills and talents than we rate ourselves, meaning there is a strength we are not fully using. That's what we call the *Ferrari in the garage* phenomenon: we have a valuable asset that is simply sitting unused in the garage.

4) **People realize they are not as good in some roles as they thought.** This is the reverse of the previous point. There are often some tasks we think we do well but that other people don't think we're so good at.

As we said earlier, we chose the Team Role model over other alternative models (some of them also excellent) partly because it provides a great deal of useful information and does so efficiently, combining a strong research-based foundation with ease of use. But we also like this model because the information and learning it provides is so valuable at both the individual and group level in terms of improving interaction effectiveness. And that's what we'll cover in the rest of this chapter.

Improving Your Personal Impact

One thing that makes finding out about Team Roles "fun" is that people get personal insights that help them interact more effectively. Here are three specific ways in which knowledge of their own Team Role strengths and weaknesses helps people.

1. Improved ability to play to strengths

There are two ways that individual strengths can be better exploited once people and their groups know about them.

The first way is that an individual will find more opportunities to play to a preferred role once their group helps them recognize it. For example, one member of a product steering committee was very frustrated because he felt like a fish out of water: as a product designer, he was the sole creative person on a team of highly analytical engineers. He'd learned not to bring up ideas because they'd just get shot down by the rest of the team. However, once the team began to realize that they benefited from using all the skills available, the other members began to welcome this designer's ideas (even the crazy ones). Many of the ideas were ultimately discarded, but some were extremely creative and provided the engineers with insights that they were able to turn into practical solutions to thorny problems.

The second type of personal insight people gain from a Team Role report is the *Ferrari in the garage* phenomenon: an individual learns to value and emphasize a strength they either didn't recognize in themselves or had undervalued. *People tend to underrate themselves in things that come easily to them (see sidebar, next page) but that are highly valued by the people around them.*

The Ferrari in the Garage Phenomenon: Undervaluing what comes easily to you

One of the issues that often arise with Team Role strengths is that people don't appreciate or recognize the value of the kinds of work that come easily to them. One woman we know, for instance, was really good at bringing a team closer together and smoothing ruffled feathers, but it came so easily to her that she didn't think that talent was anything special. However, her teammates *did* recognize and value her people skills.

The typical reaction to these situations is confusion. People think, "This is weird! What are these other people seeing that I can't see?" Once they get over the shock, they start to pay more attention to times when they are (or could be) using a talent that their team members or co-workers have recognized. The more their subsequent experience validates other people's perceptions, the more deliberate they become in using the talent to help their group.

---

2. Managing an allowable weakness

As Peter Drucker wrote, "The art of leadership is to bring out people's strengths and make their weaknesses irrelevant." The art of teamwork is the same. In our experience, what hinders personal and team effectiveness is more often an unmanaged weakness than the failure to play to a strength. Look at the allowable weaknesses column in Table A (p. 63)—surely you or someone you know has slowed down a team because they were easily preoccupied, overly analytical, indecisive, impulsive, or any of the other weaknesses listed in the table.

These weaknesses are "allowable" because they are part of a package deal; those characteristics contribute to the strength. The idea that they are an integral part of our makeup is liberating in the sense that we should not think of them as problems to be fixed. As we noted earlier, however, labeling them as "allowable" is not an excuse; that label doesn't mean you can avoid dealing with a weakness. An unmanaged allowable weakness can reach a point where it becomes dis-allowable because it harms the individual's and the group's effectiveness.

Managing your own allowable weaknesses means first acknowledging they exist and then finding ways to make sure they don't become a problem. Although this is a point of self-awareness, it is very difficult for an individual to manage a weakness entirely on their own. Besides the individual responsibility to manage a weakness, there is a group responsibility to contribute to that process. Here are three examples that illustrate this idea:

- A senior manager who scored high on the Shaper skills in the Team Role evaluation was known as a strong personality who really understood the company and could deliver results. But if you review Table A, you'll see that people with these strengths can tend to come across as impatient and insensitive. They can state opinions in ways that make it sound as if they don't want to hear any arguments (even if that is not the case). This manager realized that she would need to think carefully about using her people skills more deliberately in order to soften the impact of her sometimes-forceful assertions, and also become attuned to the impact her behavior had on others. Her management team agreed that if she came across strongly they would give her the benefit of the doubt about her intent and speak up if her questions felt like an interrogation.

- A middle manager in a product development group was not surprised to learn that he scored high in the Plant skills— someone who is very creative. But he had a tendency to not really listen to other people's ideas, and could become absorbed in what was right in front of his face (ignoring other priorities). For his part, he agreed to be more patient in listening to ideas brought to him and developed a new habit of checking his priorities regularly. His team agreed to speak up if they thought he was getting sidetracked and get better at their own advocacy skills to make sure the manager really heard their ideas.

- There was a woman that teams liked to work with because of her Implementer skills (she was great at developing action plans). But sometimes they became frustrated because she was inflexible and did not appreciate last minute changes. She was, for instance, slow in adopting new technology and tended to stick to her tried-and-true way of doing things. To make sure this inflexibility did not harm her or her team's effectiveness, this woman had to become much more conscious about not being judgmental when her co-workers had free-flowing discussions that to her seemed off course. She also specifically asked her teams to point out when they perceived her as being inflexible, and her team members agreed to give her as much advance notice as possible when they knew a change was coming. This has helped encourage more creativity on her teams, and they've seen much better results from their collaboration.

3. Improving an individual's versatility

As we noted above, most people will have several most-preferred roles as well as several manageable roles (those where they rated middle-of-the road). Versatility at an individual level comes from knowing which preferred role to play to in any situation along with being able to flex into a manageable role if it would help the group. Using skills related to a manageable role doesn't come as naturally to people as playing to their most-preferred roles, but they can usually become competent at it.

Being able to adjust in this way can greatly improve a person's management and leadership competency and their ability to effectively manage different situations and challenges. Here is an example of how individual versatility can benefit a team:

> One team we worked with lacked anyone with strong Coordinator skills—so the team struggled to reach consensus and gain alignment around their goals and actions. Most of the team rated very poorly in Coordinator skills, but one woman's ratings were in the middle. While not particularly strong in those skills, she was better at it than anyone else on the team. So she started to consciously focus on coordination. Doing so was uncomfortable at first, but the team supported her efforts and didn't expect her to be perfect. Gradually her ability to execute this role improved. The team became more effective because there were fewer tasks that were overlooked or duplicated. (Plus, the woman gained valuable experience that later on made her a more effective manager.)

Team Improvement (The Power of Team Maps)

Improving individual effectiveness and versatility is just the first level of impact from understanding Team Roles. Even greater benefit comes when a group understands the mix of Team Role strengths and weaknesses represented by its members.

The simplest way to get a good picture of the group composition is by creating a table we call a Team Map (Figure 10, next page) that shows the Team Role strengths and weaknesses of all team members. These charts are quite easy to construct; the team simply creates a list of all team members then colors in the cells that correspond to each person's rating in each role. (We are restricted to using shades of black and gray here, but in real life we use green squares for the most preferred roles and red squares for the least preferred.)

Figure 10: Map of Team Roles

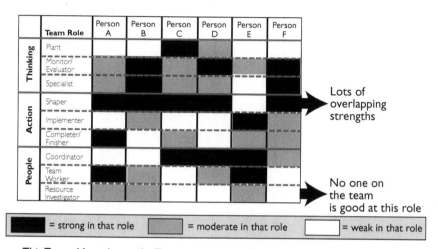

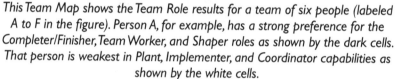

This Team Map shows the Team Role results for a team of six people (labeled A to F in the figure). Person A, for example, has a strong preference for the Completer/Finisher, Team Worker, and Shaper roles as shown by the dark cells. That person is weakest in Plant, Implementer, and Coordinator capabilities as shown by the white cells.

Learning to decipher a Team Map is straightforward. There are just three rules:

Rule 1: Have people play to their strong roles as much as possible.
For the most part, you want people to use the skills that come most naturally to them. You also want to avoid having people trying to play to their weakest (least-preferred) roles because that will just set them (and the team) up for failure. Assigning a particular task to someone who will hate it and won't be good at it is a waste of time and effort. Teams who do this flounder; there is likely to be churn as people struggle to do work they aren't really suited to. The Team Map helps the team avoid the problem of inappropriate assignments by documenting who will be good at (or at least adequate in) which kinds of work.

Example: The easy calls for the team in Figure 10 is to look at the three roles where there is only one black cell (meaning only one person is strong in the Plant, Implementer, and Completer/Finisher roles). That doesn't mean those people have to bear all the burden of performing the kinds of work associated with those roles, but the team should try to use their natural talents in those areas.

Rule 2: Decide how to deal with too much strength in any one role. As with many things in life, too much of a good thing is often a problem. Having too many people trying to fill the same Team Role is like that. It more often hinders the team than helps it.

Example: Five of the six members of the team in Figure 10 are very strong in the Shaper role. People with good Shaper skills are desirable because they bring energy to a team; so you *want* Shaper skills on your team because they help keep a team moving forward. However, people with Shaper strengths often have strong feelings, can be impatient for results, and can be viewed as being pushy. The danger for the team in Figure 10 is that the Shaper-talented members could get locked into arguments that prevent the team from making progress.

Teams that know where potential conflicts lie should do what they can to avoid the problem and have plans for reacting if the conflict does arise. In the team here, for example, the people with the overlapping strengths should consider focusing more on the skills associated with their other roles. (More on this later in the chapter.)

Rule 3: Decide how to compensate for gaps (roles where no one is strong). The other pattern to look for on a Team Map is roles where there are NO strengths (in our version that means no black cells in a given row).

Example: The team in Figure 10 has no black (meaning no strengths) in the Resource Investigator role. It would appear that no one on the team would naturally gravitate to reaching out to make connections with people outside the team, or at least would find it a burden to do so. This void could pose problems because the team would be more prone to having an inward focus, possibly becoming insular and/or failing to communicate or manage external contacts effectively. The good news for this team is that three people scored at least moderately in the Resource Investigator role; it's a manageable role for them, so they could be called upon to stretch themselves to fill that role when it's needed by the team.

Using Team Maps to become more productive

A Team Map is a surprisingly powerful way of creating team understanding on how to get the most out of all the individual resources on the team by mitigating predictable issues.

For example, consider Person C and Person D from Figure 10—we've excerpted those columns in Figure 11. We'll call these people Carla and Duane. We've worked with enough teams to know what is likely to happen between people who have profiles like Carla and Duane. Carla will push ideas forcefully on the team, thinking they are all great ideas that should be put into action immediately. Duane will cringe internally every time Carla comes up with one of her ideas because it will be very obvious to him that those ideas are usually very difficult and costly to implement. It's likely Carla and Duane will have argued frequently over what Duane sees as Carla's foolhardy rush to implement impractical ideas or about what Carla sees as Duane being obstructionist because he lacks any creative spark.

Figure 11:Team Map Excerpt

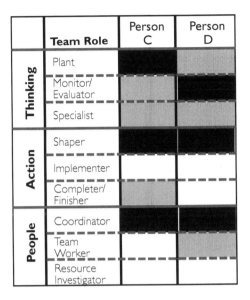

The tension between these two people is completely predictable because of the differences in their mindsets and skills. As you can see in Figure 11, Carla and Duane share two strengths (in the Shaper and Coordinator roles) but are at opposite ends of the spectrum on two Thinking roles: Carla has strong Plant skills (a creative person who plants ideas) and is poor at the Monitor/Evaluator tasks (evaluating the consequences of ideas). Duane is the exact opposite—strong in Monitor/Evaluator skills and weak in Plant skills.

If Carla and Duane could be taught about the Team Roles and shown the Team Map, they would have a framework for talking about their differences in neutral terms. Duane could acknowledge Carla's Plant tendencies without having to say she has some crazy ideas; Carla could recognize Duane's ability to soberly evaluate ideas without calling him obstructionist. They would also both recognize that their different approaches are perfectly normal *and needed by their team*—and then talk about ways to make sure those differences were an asset not a roadblock. For example, Carla could bounce her ideas off Duane before the meetings so that they could present only the workable ones to the team.

In short, a Team Map gives the individuals on a team a starting point for talking about ways they can work together more effectively.[4]

Adaptation: Compensating for imbalances

Forewarned is forearmed, as the saying goes. And a Team Map helps arm teams with knowledge that will help them adjust for the particular mix of strengths and weaknesses on their team. In fact, the Team Role research led to the conclusion that the difference between a team's success and failure was not whether it was perfectly balanced in terms of the representation of Team Roles (meaning at least one person is strong in each role), but rather *how well the team learned to adjust situationally and compensate for any imbalances.*

For a team to have a strong bias towards one category of Team Roles is not unusual; perhaps its members all come from the same work area and were hired for a particular set of similar skills. Just as one example, we often see teams that like to get things done (multiple people on the team have strong Action skills). They are excellent at getting items checked off their To Do lists, but sometimes have to revisit their decisions because the actions weren't well thought out. Here's an example:

> *A team assigned to review and improve its company's customer service policies was frustrated. The team had been meeting periodically for months and found themselves starting over almost from scratch at every meeting. There were plenty of ideas flowing but it was hard for the team to decide which ideas were worth pursuing and which were not. If they started*

---

4 To learn more about how Team Maps are constructed and interpreted, see the example with commentary at www2.3circlepartners.com/interaction-gap-resources.

to converge on an idea, someone would come up with some-thing entirely new to be considered.

After examining its Team Map, the team realized that there was a preponderance of people with strong Thinking skills among the members. People with these strengths often love spending time analyzing data and information, discussing options, looking for new ideas, and so on. But they may be less interested in making the ideas a reality! To improve pro-ductivity, the team had to look at ways to draw on secondary strengths that various team members had in the Action and People roles. They discussed their situation and made several decisions on how they would address their team's tendencies. This resulted in a set of ground rules about when to call a halt to analysis and push for decisions and actions.

The Joy of Personal and Group Effectiveness

When people see their Team Role report for the first time, there is almost always an "aha" moment when they realize something important about themselves that they hadn't known before but rings true. The same is true when teams create a Team Map. They understand why certain types of work—coming up with ideas, turning ideas into action, or working collaboratively—are either very difficult or very easy for them. More importantly, they have the data that helps them compensate for gaps and use each team member's talents to the fullest. And that's what makes for great interaction and better results.

The logic of having people identify and work on their strengths is unassailable, but the benefits of using the Team Role model and its impact go far beyond what we can portray on the written page:

- We can't capture the energy and enthusiasm that comes when people understand more about what they are good at (and what they aren't).

- We can't adequately capture the relief that comes when people understand they can't possibly be great in all nine Team Roles, or when they recognize that something they thought of as a fault can't be eliminated but can be managed as an allowable weakness.

- We can't depict the speed with which people begin to improve when they can focus on work that plays to their strengths. (All of us find it easier to improve in areas where we are naturally talented.)

You may want to use the specific Team Role model in this chapter, or you may not. Either way, the principle we're advocating is finding a framework that helps people understand how they can best contribute to the work of a group—and vice versa, enables groups and teams to know how to best use the talents of their members. Building that knowledge within the team is very freeing and plays a big role in avoiding the fatal flaws. Because people will be playing to their strengths more often, you will run into less defensiveness. Whatever model you use should be built around the combination of self-awareness and group involvement that the Team Role model uses, so that you can simultaneously create a shared vocabulary around interaction and get everyone shaping new norms for the group.

Mundane I– Conquering the Meeting Beast

Could anything be more mundane than meetings? They are the most obvious form of interaction in most organizations, and something most of us experience nearly every day. They are also a fundamental forum through which the work of management (and leadership) takes place.

Because meetings are such an inescapable and increasing staple of business life, you would think that the techniques for holding good meetings should be so well-entrenched that bad meetings would be the exception. Unfortunately, the reverse seems to be true. All of us have been to countless meetings that felt like a waste of time, and whenever we poll our customers, 80–90% say they are dissatisfied with the productivity of their meetings.

This discrepancy between theory and reality is a mystery. The techniques for holding good meetings are not rocket science; it doesn't take advanced degrees to do it well. There are some simple, basic methods that have been documented for decades.

Nonetheless, problems with meetings appear to be rampant. Companies of all kinds have meeting challenges, no matter what their culture or industry. Yet oddly enough, nearly everyone we talk to, and especially experienced managers and executives, are able to describe what it takes to run a good meeting. So what gives?

In this chapter, we'll talk about some of the biggest and most common problems with meetings, and hopefully give you a few ideas for conquering this most mundane but also most critical aspect of interaction.

Start With the "Why?"

We were asked by a senior management team in a financial institution to help them understand why their monthly half-day meetings were such a struggle. To give you a taste of what went on, Figure 12 shows the outcome for all 43 topics discussed in just one of these meetings.

Figure 12: The Outcome of 43 Topics

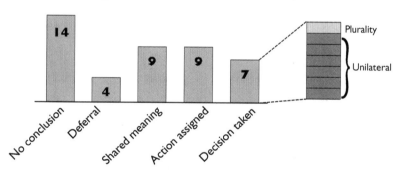

What do you think about this team's meeting effectiveness? The data is a little ambiguous. The fact that this team had the ambitious goal of handling 43 different issues in one meeting is an early indicator of problems to come (how many times have you been frustrated in a meeting because the agenda was crammed full of topics?). To understand what's happening here, we have to dig a little deeper.

The first three outcomes reading left to right in Figure 12 could be either legitimate outcomes or an indication of poor decision making depending on the circumstances:

- **No conclusion** and **deferral** are acceptable options if the group realizes it doesn't have the right people or the right information to take action. Better no decision than the wrong decision. But they are poor outcomes if the group is simply avoiding more conclusive actions or trying to pass the buck onto someone else, or if the problem with a lack of information has occurred before and was never addressed. If the problem is a lack of information, that calls into question the quality of preparation for the meeting. As it turned out, these were usually undesirable outcomes for the executive team because the group would repeatedly back off from making decisions about some issues.

- A **shared meaning** around a concept or initiative is almost always a good thing, especially among the top leaders of an organization. Without a shared understanding, people or groups can go off in different directions, which leads to misalignment (a problem we'll tackle in the next chapter). However, if the group has to repeatedly reach a shared understanding of the same topic, that is not a good pattern. Neither is reaching a shared understanding if there is no improved outcome as a consequence. (For the most part, a shared understanding was a good outcome for this team.)

The last two outcomes on the chart—**actions assigned** and **decisions taken**—are often the reasons why teams come together in the first place, so both those options are also good choices in the right circumstances. However, take a look at the "decision taken" breakout box in Figure 12: 6 out of 7 times, the boss made a unilateral decision. You might think he was simply over-exerting his authority, but what happened in reality was that the boss became so frustrated by analysis paralysis and constant deferral of issues that he felt compelled to make a call so the group could claim it accomplished *something* in the meeting.

What this data helps demonstrate is that groups can waste a lot of time if they are not clear about the purpose of a meeting. Why are people spending their time in a meeting and what do you want to accomplish? That in turn will help you decide the best way to achieve your goals.

This leads to the first two guidelines for dealing with topic overload or a lack of action:

- Define the type of meeting and degree or quality of interaction that is required:
    - Status meetings (low interaction)
    - Routine or day-to-day tactical work (medium)
    - Complex problem solving and strategic decision making (high)
- Hold separate meetings for the three types of meetings; don't try and mix them.
    - If little to no interaction is required, consider *not having the meeting!* Use other ways to communicate the information.
    - Split out strategy meetings (longer, less frequent, higher degree of interaction) from tactical meetings (shorter, more frequent, medium interaction).
    - Split out large group communication/update meetings from small group decision-making meetings.

Last but not least, the simplest but biggest-impact change you can make in your meetings is to have an **outcome orientation**. What does that mean? Let's look first at what usually happens. When we ask people to tell us why they are pulled into meetings, we hear answers like:

- Review staffing reports

- Give status reports on projects

- Evaluate new data that has come in

- Assess risks

- Review options on the new product design

- Present the findings of legal reviews

Sounds typical, doesn't it? The problem is that all of these statements describe topics or activities, not specific outcomes the group wants to produce. If you make only one change based on this chapter, make it this: identify the purpose of each meeting (and each agenda item) by defining the specific outcome you want. One technique for making sure you are thinking about an outcome is to say: "At the end of this meeting, we will have _____."

For example, here's the same list as above, but this time with a clear outcome identified for each issue:

We will have:

- A document outlining adjusted staffing levels for next quarter

- An agreed priority ranking of projects

- A decision on whether to change the customer satisfaction survey based on new data

- An updated risk-mitigation plan

- A decision on the rank of the five options for the new product design based on criteria decided at our previous meeting

- A list of compliance training priorities based on legal reviews

After the executive team reviewed the data on outcomes from its meeting (Figure 12), we reviewed these principles with them. All of the executives realized that they had been trying to accomplish too many different things in one meeting. So they decided unanimously to have two distinct types of meetings: tactical meetings held every two to three weeks, and strategic meetings no more than monthly.

The executives also began defining much clearer outcomes for each meeting as well (for example, describing the required type of resolution for each tactical issue). Having a defined outcome made it easier for the team to do a check at the end of their meetings: "Did we accomplish this outcome or not?" If not, they were then able to learn from the experience and carry the learning forward to the next meeting thereby creating a culture of continuous improvement.

There was even more work for this executive team, which we'll talk about next.

Match the Who (and How Many) to the Why

When working with the executive team introduced in the previous section, we also shot video and then analyzed the interaction patterns from several meetings. Figure 13 shows a typical analysis of participation for this team, which happened to have 11 members. The data represents the percentage of meeting time that each person was talking (their airtime).

As you can see, 6 of the 11 people on this team contributed very little. That raises the obvious question: *Why were these people in the room at all?*

Figure 13: Airtime of Executive Meeting Participants

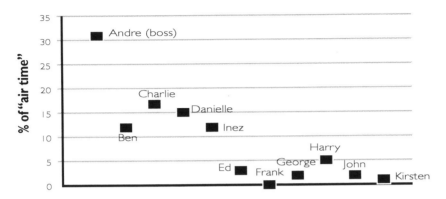

The most benign interpretation would be that those members were there only to listen and learn, but that seems unlikely because this pattern appeared regularly. Plus, these were all experienced executives, not new hires or junior managers who would benefit from regular exposure to executive activities. Surely there are better uses for six experienced managers than having them sit nearly silent during half-day meetings!

There are other interpretations of this pattern, all of which indicate major gaps in interaction. If these managers were there because they had relevant information to impart, then they never fulfilled that purpose because they rarely spoke! If that was the case, then there's another critical question: *Why was participation so imbalanced?* Was the boss so enamored of his own voice that he rarely let others speak? Were the non-talkers simply not as assertive as those who contributed more?

The team took two steps to resolve the participation issue:

- First, they became more deliberate about which executives should attend which meetings (which became especially important once they began having separate tactical and strategic meetings).

- Second, they started emphasizing basic facilitation techniques to create more balanced participation during the meetings.

Let's explore more around why these choices were good for this team.

Being deliberate about meeting attendance

Time and time again, we've seen firsthand that it doesn't work to have a decision-making meeting where there are too many people present (anything above 8 is too many). If the meeting's purpose is to solve a problem or reach a decision, aim to have at least 3 to 4 people present but no more than 6. In our experience, that size of group is large enough to have fruitful discussions but not so large that it's difficult to make a decision. (If you need to have more than 6 people—or at a stretch 7—in problem-solving or decision-making meetings, we strongly urge you to divide the big group into subgroups for the discussion, then come back together for a report out—and have a final group discussion to reach agreement.)

If there is less interaction required, you can go higher on the number of participants. For more information on the impact that team size has on the effectiveness of the work they do, see our article, "Teamwork — Team Size Matters!" (available on our website).

The executive team members agreed that all 11 people should be present at status meetings (so people could ask questions), but they would limit the size for all other meetings with only a few exceptions. If there were strategy issues that needed input from all 11 people, either the team leader (Andre) would meet separately with smaller groups then present a consensus decision to the full team, or the full team would split into small groups in separate rooms to discuss the issue then come back together to report out and reach a decision. Attendance at the new tactical meetings varied every time depending on the purpose.

Striving for better participation

Separating out the purpose and limiting the size of the meetings helped this executive team, but there was still uneven participation in some meetings.

They knew this was a problem because they had all gone through the decision-making simulation we discussed in Chapter 1 and seen that in the first few rounds *someone* in the group had the right answer, but the group settled on a wrong answer because:

- No one had asked the person with the right answer to share their ideas.

- The person chose not to speak up.

- The group heard the right answer (that is, the person spoke up) but dismissed it—perhaps the loudest person or someone with more power or expertise was pushing the wrong answers and the rest of the group acquiesced.

The realization that people with the right answers or relevant information aren't speaking up or aren't being heard leads to another phenomenon we observe during our courses: About 70% of participants are eventually given feedback that they need to speak up more and be more assertive. The remaining 30% hear feedback to the effect that, while their contributions are valued, they should do more listening and inquiry—that is, actively and purposefully involve others in the discussion.

A reaction we sometimes get when we discuss this "talker vs. listener" dynamic is the idea that "silence means consent." People think it's up to the quieter folks to speak up. That doesn't work for the same reason that it doesn't work to tell the talkers to sit quietly throughout a meeting. It goes against their nature.

Once a team recognizes that it has to work hard to get all ideas, good and bad, on the table, basic facilitation skills become more important as do inquiry and listening skills. In general, you should work to develop sufficient skills within your groups so that most meeting facilitation is handled by the group itself. However, in some circumstances (such as those involving intense conflict), it may help to have someone not on the team perform the function of facilitator. The facilitator's job is to pay attention to the meeting process more so than the content. He or she should make sure that the group understands the purpose of each agenda item and the process that will be used to cover that item (open discussion, structured discussion, presentation and analysis, etc.). The facilitator also should make sure the group makes deliberate decisions about its use of meeting time—for example, if an agenda item is running long, does the group want to continue the discussion and sacrifice time on another item or table it for another meeting? (Being able to contribute to a meeting that you are also trying to facilitate is a difficult balance to achieve, but is something that all truly high-performance teams master.)

Besides trying to balance out participation, a team can be more flexible when everyone has basic facilitation skills. For example, a project team was having a conference call meeting when the person who called the meeting said right up front, "I can't manage the meeting *and* contribute to the discussion as well. Can someone else facilitate?" Another person stepped in and helped guide the discussion.

Now, we're *not* saying that a good meeting is one where everyone has the same amount of airtime, but you want to make sure you've elicited all relevant information and ideas and given them proper consideration. For example:

The leadership team at a Midwest-based company had several members that were very strong in the action-oriented Team Roles. But there were two members who were strong in the thinking roles and they were by far the most creative people and quietest people on the team.

When the team realized this was the case, they became better at creating space in the meeting for the quieter people to speak up—meaning the managers would directly solicit the opinions of the creative people and wait in silence (if necessary) until they were able to articulate their ideas. This required an adjustment from the action-oriented team members, but was well worth the effort. Within a few months of making these changes, the team came up with a new product that is now turning out to be a major success for this company. The executive in charge is convinced that it was ideas provided by the two quieter team members that led to this new product.

All of these lessons about meeting participation held true for the executive team whose data we showed previously, and they took steps to emphasize basic facilitation and participation skills. The starting point was to have the group focus on improving its inquiry skills (asking questions and listening to understand) and advocacy skills (speaking up clearly and providing data that support assumptions and positions so the person's ideas are clearly understood). Because they were fighting the "gravity of habit," the team recognized it would take sustained effort to build new patterns of interaction. One technique they adopted was doing an inquiry/advocacy check at the end of meetings ("On a scale of 1 to 10, how well did we do with inquiry? What about advocacy?"). Another technique is to have an outsider sit in on some meetings to provide the team with objective input.

Keep It Simple and Practical

Being clear about the purpose of a meeting (that is, defining a specific outcome you want to produce) and which people need to be present to contribute to the purpose eliminates wasted meeting time. Beyond those crucial steps, good meetings are often a matter of keeping your methods simple and practical. We have two tips to get you started.

1. Adopt simple, flexible standards

In some companies, the meeting norm is that people show up more or less at a specific time, online or in person, and then everyone figures out what's going to happen in that meeting. That works well for some people but can be very frustrating for others.

Other organizations have a much more structured approach to meetings, requiring that people fill in agenda templates with assigned responsibilities, estimated times, and desired outcomes for every agenda item.

Neither of these approaches is right or wrong. We summarize our philosophy as follows:

Too little structure = Chaos
Too much structure = Stifled contributions
Just enough structure = Liberates!

In other words, the best meeting structure for you is the one that works for a particular purpose and accommodates the needs of the participants.

Free-form meetings can work if there is a clear purpose and the right people are involved (meaning those whose participation is required to achieve the purpose), but if they are too free-form, people can become disgruntled wondering why they are in the room. Structured meetings work for situations where multiple topics need be covered efficiently in a limited timeframe and with large groups. But imposing too much structure at times when it's not needed will lead people to dismiss the practice as ineffective. Some people thrive on wide-ranging divergent discussions; others are driven crazy by that lack of structure.

That is why it helps to have a flexible approach to meetings that adapts not only to the problem at hand but also to the styles of the players involved and the culture in which the meeting is taking place.

In the "just enough structure = liberates!" category, several years ago our company adopted a planning method for our internal meetings that was simple, effective, and flexible. We call this format the **3Ps**, for Purpose, Process, and Preparation.

1. **Purpose:** What you would like to get out of your meeting. As discussed above, the purpose must be stated as a desired outcome.

2. **Process:** The process that will be used in the meeting. Is it an open discussion? A presentation? Brainstorming to solicit ideas? Analysis and voting to help the group converge on a decision? (The description of the process can often include the agenda for the meeting.)

3. **Preparation**: What participants should do before arriving at the meeting. Do they need to review prior information or decisions? Read a new file? Have some questions framed in their minds? It may be helpful to create some context for the meeting as part of the information provided prior to the meeting.

Laying out the 3Ps before a meeting works because it gives people time to reflect prior to the meeting and to understand why they're attending it. When we survey our clients, there are invariably people who find that establishing purpose and process on the spot in the meeting is very uncomfortable. They contribute much better to the discussion if they have some time to mull over the issues in their minds before the meeting.

This framework has helped our own meetings tremendously, and we highly recommend you explore making the 3Ps a norm for every meeting. It is simple enough that it places a minimal burden on the people organizing the meetings, but still flexible enough to accommodate a wide range of meeting structures. That combination of structure and flexibility makes the 3Ps useful in many circumstances, as illustrated by the following example:

> *Eric needed to get his thoughts together about the upcoming sales manager quarterly meeting and plan an agenda. Since he knew that planning wasn't his strongest point, he decided to reach out to a colleague, Nancy, for help. He spent about 5 minutes writing her an email (Figure 14).*

Figure 14: 3Ps for the Meeting to Develop the Plan

TO: Nancy@ABCcompany.com
From: Eric@ABCcompany.com

Need your help again on formulating an agenda for the upcoming quarterly sales meeting. Can we get together?

Purpose: A completed set of goals, an agenda, and prep work necessary to make the meeting happen.

Process: Let's review the previous meetings agenda, goals etc. Spend about an hour working together: making sure we are agreed on purpose, then brainstorming ideas and come to consensus. Afterwards, I'll send out the agenda to participants.

Preparation: Please review our sales strategy document prior to the meeting if you have a chance. That way we can hit the ground running (I've attached the latest version to save you retrieval time). I'll ask our admins to work together to find a suitable time for a meeting.

> *Three days later Eric and Nancy met. They spent the full hour as he had suggested and came up with the following 3P-style outline for the quarterly meeting:*

Figure 15: 3Ps for Quarterly Agenda Email

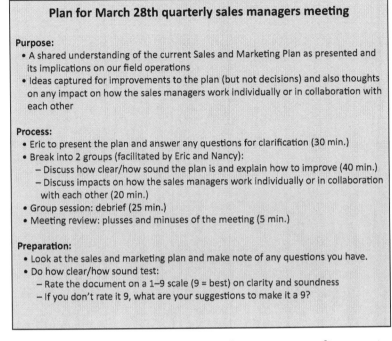

Plan for March 28th quarterly sales managers meeting

Purpose:
- A shared understanding of the current Sales and Marketing Plan as presented and its implications on our field operations
- Ideas captured for improvements to the plan (but not decisions) and also thoughts on any impact on how the sales managers work individually or in collaboration with each other

Process:
- Eric to present the plan and answer any questions for clarification (30 min.)
- Break into 2 groups (facilitated by Eric and Nancy):
    - Discuss how clear/how sound the plan is and explain how to improve (40 min.)
    - Discuss impacts on how the sales managers work individually or in collaboration with each other (20 min.)
- Group session: debrief (25 min.)
- Meeting review: plusses and minuses of the meeting (5 min.)

Preparation:
- Look at the sales and marketing plan and make note of any questions you have.
- Do how clear/how sound test:
    - Rate the document on a 1–9 scale (9 = best) on clarity and soundness
    - If you don't rate it 9, what are your suggestions to make it a 9?

The organization that Eric works for runs most of its meetings in this manner. They report that since they have adopted the 3Ps approach, their meeting times have dropped by 30% and they have documented cases of much better decision making.

Many organizations have told us that they find it relatively easy to follow the 3P framework because it is simple common sense. We won't argue with that.

2. Improve task assignments

Meeting frustration arises often when group members don't complete work they were assigned or at least don't do it very well. Naturally, a lack of organizational skills could contribute here, but oftentimes issues in this area could be linked to assigning work to someone without considering their interaction strengths and weaknesses. As we talked about in Chapter 4, people will differ in their ability to coordinate activities, follow through on details, present and analyze data, think in terms of processes, read body language, and on and on. Assigning someone a task that plays to their weak roles will very likely lead to poor motivation to complete the task, possible procrastination, and poor execution—a recipe for failure.

To avoid this kind of problem, engage team members and take into consideration their Team Roles when assigning tasks.

When the Simple Is Hard

A leadership team discovered that people often had differ-ent memories of decisions made in its meetings. They would argue over what conclusions were made, even if issues and decisions were documented in the meeting notes. So the team decided that they needed to make better use of visual aids (white boards, flipcharts) to capture key points and decisions during a meeting and make sure everyone agreed with the way the decision was worded and what it meant.

They practiced this new habit faithfully for one or two meetings under the observation of an outside facilitator with great results. But when we visited them six months later, the team leader said, "Uh oh. I guess we'd better get the flipcharts out." Clearly that new practice had died away quickly after the facilitator's influence was removed, even though the team had agreed on the practice and seen the benefits.

For this leadership team, better visual management was a new thing. As it happened, the team didn't meet for a month or two after those initial sessions, so the habit of using visuals never had time to develop. After the break, the leader wasn't consistent in applying the new method and some people on the team were resistant to change (a characteristic of some Team Roles). One member of the team viewed it as a distraction from all the real work the team had to complete.

Finding the energy and commitment to pay attention to something as mundane as improving your meeting techniques is a challenge that every team must solve for itself. This flipchart-challenged leadership team brought back the facilitator for one meeting to refresh everyone's understanding of what visual techniques were available and how it would help them get more done. They then realized that one of the team members was actually very good at thinking visually and she agreed to become the champion of the practice. Their third step was to add a standard check-in item at the end of each meeting: "How well did we use visuals?"

Ultimately, it took more than a year until the use of visual tools became second nature to this leadership team—and this was something the team had agreed was helpful! But don't think badly of this leadership team or view them as incompetent. Their experience is typical of what we see in the real world. Changing norms of any kind is very difficult; changing meeting norms may sound simple but is extremely difficult to accomplish.

Continually Learn to Improve Your Meetings

As we've said, all the techniques described in this chapter are simple to understand but not easy to implement. Being persistent in focusing on simple meeting techniques increases the odds that they will become norms:

- Consistently using a simple meeting structure and making sure you and your groups make a point of actively facilitating your meetings goes a long way towards improving the effectiveness of your time together. People will know *why* they are in the room (or on the phone) and what it is they are expected to contribute.

- Having the group define and enforce ground rules is a way to engage group members in shaping the kind of meeting experience they want to have. Plus it gives them a stake in establishing interaction-supportive norms that the whole group embraces. (Once again, you are building both individual and group skills.)

- Use of meeting ground rules, such as "everybody gets a chance to speak" or "we will always look at what the data says," can help avoid problems with imbalanced influence on the team. It also creates a safer environment where people will be more comfortable expressing their ideas—which can minimize the potential for strong emotions or defensiveness to sidetrack your meetings.

Think of these suggestions as starting points; the solutions for meeting problems have to be customized to the need and the team. To get started, you might want to work with the other participants in a meeting that needs improvement, and identify the problem that is harming interaction effectiveness the most. Is it a lack of an outcome focus? No facilitation skills? Poor work assignments? Identify a technique you think will help you solve that problem, and focus on solving that one problem before tackling another. Don't expect instantaneous results—as the examples in previous sections illustrate, it can take a while for even very simple techniques to replace old norms.

To make the practice more interesting, set goals for your groups around meeting effectiveness. Do a check to see how well you're doing against your goals at the end of every meeting initially, and then periodically afterwards. We often do a simple, "What worked? What didn't work?" check at the end of meetings, but there are also more formal, structured ways to evaluate your team's effectiveness.[5]

You may also want to check out our article "Treat Meetings as an Ongoing Process, Not Isolated Events" (on our website) for further ideas on establishing more productive meetings that can help your organization become more effective.

---

5 See, for example, our Interaction Index, available on our website at
www2.3circlepartners.com/interaction-gap-resources.

—6—

Mundane 2 – Walking the Talk on Alignment

Whenever we hear about post mortems that teams do to figure out why they struggled so much or why they failed to produce promised deliverables, we hear statements like:

- We never really defined roles and responsibilities. As a result, there was duplication of effort.

- We received different information depending on which manager we talked to, so we often had to do a lot of rework.

- Everyone seemed to interpret our mission differently, so we experienced scope creep.

- "Those guys" (on the other team) made decisions they weren't supposed to make.

- We wasted energy on blaming and finger pointing when mistakes occurred.

- We made up the rules along the way. Had we sat down at the beginning of the project and discussed possible barriers, we would have spent much less time resolving issues during the project.

- It took us a long time to gel as a team, but once we did start working together it was amazing what we accomplished.

- We agreed we were aligned in general, but not on the details or specifics.

These kinds of situations are incredibly common. The root cause of them all? A lack of alignment. Or perhaps a better way to put it is "unrecognized misalignment." More often than not, people or groups who are supposedly working toward a shared goal will be misaligned in some fundamental way. They will have different interpretations of priorities, decisions, responsibilities, processes . . . or any of many more factors that affect how well they can collaborate.

Surely you have been in misalignment situations yourself. Perhaps you can recall a meeting where everyone seemed to have agreed on a decision, yet it later turned out each person had a different idea about what they said yes to. Or maybe you really *were* aligned in the meeting, but afterwards new information or changing conditions changed people's interpretation. However it happened, once the trajectories were shifted, the differences in interpretations moved farther and farther apart, and your once-aligned people or groups ended up working at cross purposes. No one can interact effectively when they are aimed in different directions.

Just as with the abundance of poor meetings, the frequency of misalignment is somewhat mystifying because alignment is a common topic of discussion. It's rare these days to find a manager or group leader who isn't aware of the importance of alignment, which is why a discussion of purpose and goals is often the first thing on the agenda for the kickoff of any big meeting, major engagement, or project team.

Trouble is, alignment between people or groups is just like the alignment on your car: the wheels do not suddenly jump into alignment; it takes effort to make it happen. Plus, once aligned, wear and tear or a big pothole can easily shift the wheels out of alignment. The same thing happens in the workplace. Gaining up-front alignment is harder than people realize because of all the pieces that have to be aligned, and any alignment you achieve *will* drift into misalignment unless you are proactive in maintaining it.

As you can tell from the mundane label on this chapter, getting aligned and staying aligned requires ongoing effort, more so than insights or innovation. In this chapter, we'll talk about how to make sure your groups or teams are truly aligned and what it will take to keep them aligned.

Misalignment Creep

When people mention alignment, most often they mean getting people headed towards the same goal or at least in the same direction. Certainly that is important but you have to take your up-front alignment discussion much deeper if you want to avoid problems down the road because there are many, many ways in which people can be misaligned.

Here is a quick example to illustrate this point:

> One day a few years back, a new regional sales director visited the head office of his company and made some comments that inadvertently resulted in getting the regional operations director into trouble with his boss. Naturally, the operations director was not happy. After the sales director returned to the regional office, he went to talk to the operations director and explained that it was an honest mistake—he just hadn't realized that his remarks would reflect badly on the regional operations group.
>
> To avoid any recurrence of this situation, the two agreed to a guiding principle going forward: neither would surprise the other with something they were going to report to the head office. Of course, they didn't always see eye to eye, so some

of their future conversations started off with "You're not going to like this, but here's what I need to report to the head office next week...." Committing to this guiding principle helped the two maintain a productive relationship built on trust.

These managers were strategically aligned in the sense of both wanting to support increased sales for the company. But they realized that if they wanted to work together effectively, they had to agree on "rules of the game" to guide how they would achieve the goal. In other words, they added **tactical alignment** onto their strategic alignment. Tactical alignment defines how people and groups will work together in their day-to-day environment, which of course includes clearly defining the rules of interaction.

The lack of tactical alignment is one of the most common causes of unrecognized misalignment that we see. In fact, most of the examples given at the start of this chapter were forms of tactical misalignment: people had different interpretations of ground rules, processes, roles, responsibilities, accountabilities, etc. Moreover, misalignment on these issues can overshadow any alignment that does exist. Sometimes, the way out of this kind of mess is to start by revisiting the goal, as we'll discuss next.

Using Tactical Alignment to Break Icy Ground

If you are trying to align people or groups who have a history of conflict or have been isolated in different silos for so long that they don't know how to begin, we suggest you start by having them work through tactical alignment issues. What will the group ground rules be? How will the group do its work? Who will be responsible for what?

This kind of interactional alignment is, of course, necessary for the smooth operation of the group. But it also serves the purpose of getting people to talk about generally non-contentious issues before they have to confront the hard stuff. Few people have such strong feelings around issues like "meetings will start on time" that they will get into an argument over it. Working through these easier issues gets the group members into the habit of cooperating with each other.

Realignment: What's In It For Us?

One of the biggest challenges of up-front alignment around a goal or purpose is that this kind of alignment **cannot be imposed**. Yes, sometimes a leader will tell staff what it is they are supposed to do or what goal or strategy they should shoot for. Unfortunately when some executives use the term "get aligned" what they really mean is that they want their people to "fall in line" behind a directive. They assume that if they are VERY clear about the goal, then people will happily fall in line to support it. That assumption misses the underlying truth that commitment needs communication, and real communication is a dialogue. Monologues, however well delivered, can only get compliance—and compliance at best is a mediocre goal and often represents nothing more than passive resistance.

To contribute to the kind of effective interaction we're talking about in this book, people have to see a personal motivation to support the direction. You're probably familiar with the term WIIFM—short for *What's In It for Me?*—used to represent the reasons why an individual will want to do something. WIIFM is an important element in creating effective interaction because the people or groups you want to work together have to have a reason for believing that doing so is in their best interests.

However, in our experience WIIFM only brings people to the table, it doesn't get them aligned. To make sure that people are headed in the same direction, you have to involve them in discussions in which they discover for themselves their overlapping interests—what we call WIIFU or What's In It For Us (Figure 16).

Figure 16: What's In It For Us?

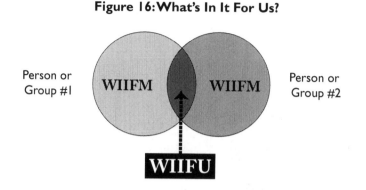

Person or Group #1 — WIIFM — WIIFM — Person or Group #2 — WIIFU

Here's an example of WIIFU at work:

A European medical equipment company had good market leadership all around the globe except in the U.S. The new CEO wanted to rectify that situation and commissioned the international marketing group (based in Europe) to work with the marketing group for the American business unit to develop and implement a new strategy.

Predictably, the two groups had very different ideas about their roles—that is, they were very misaligned around the rules of the game. The international marketing group felt their ideas should have precedence because the ultimate responsibility was theirs. The U.S. marketing group's attitude was "obviously we are here because you guys don't have any experience in the American market, so we should do things our way."

The initial exchanges (we can't really call them discussions) between these groups led to painful disagreements on which decisions each group was responsible for, what everyone's specific job description was, and the extent of each group's limits of control. However, the leaders of the two groups were determined to get the launch back on track. They decided on a series of face-to-face meetings between the groups to hammer out all the areas of disagreement.

One of the first things the leaders did when the groups met was to involve everyone in the room in helping to define what it was they had in common—what was in it for "us" not just "me"? Everyone agreed that increasing market share in the U.S. was the top priority and overarching goal of the combined team. During the rest of this meeting, with that shared goal posted prominently on a whiteboard, both groups found it far less contentious to agree on roles and responsibilities. As one member of the international team described it afterwards, "We found our discussions had shifted from arguing over who should have ownership and be in control of which task, to a discussion of which group could do the task in the most rapid and effective way. . . . In some cases we happily agreed on shared ownership."

Even more importantly, the groups decided to increase their frequency of contact to twice-monthly web meetings (one scheduled at a time inconvenient for the Europeans and the other at a time inconvenient for the Americans) as well as a quarterly face-to-face meeting, which started off with a review and reconfirmation of the shared purpose.

No substitute for old-fashioned discussions

In our experience, no group can anticipate all of the ways in which misalignment can occur. But you can avoid many problems if you deal with your rules of the game up front and then plan on making course corrections when other issues arise.

There is another important aspect of the case studies we presented above: the European and American marketing groups were able to resolve their issues only when they met face-to-face. In our experience, true alignment cannot happen through emails, texts, postings on an internet discussion page, or even phone calls. For people to become aligned with others, there has to be a true dialogue—a conversation where they have the opportunity to explain themselves, ask questions of others and get answers in real-time, suggest areas of agreement, point out flaws in others' thinking, and so on. Alignment occurs more quickly and completely through face-to-face contact, preferably in person although in today's dispersed workplaces virtual meetings with webcams can also work.

This civil division of labor around an overarching goal may seem obvious to outsiders, but we're betting that you've been locked in similar turf wars in your own company. When that happens, it's hard for the people who are arguing with each other to take a step back. Finding the common ground that everyone agrees on is an important starting point for true alignment.

Staying Aligned:
Walking the Talk Takes More Talking

In many organizations we visit, it's clear that there is a predominantly one-and-done attitude towards alignment: do it once at the beginning and you're set to go. The fallacy of that attitude should be clear by now. As we noted above, it's impossible to predict all the ways in which people and groups can be misaligned. Also, it's clear that even once-aligned people or groups will drift out of alignment, sometimes quite rapidly. Checking alignment cannot be a one-time event; it has to be monitored and checked with a greater frequency than is taking place now in most organizations.

That switch in attitude brings about dramatic shifts in behavior. Once people realize they need to assume that misalignment is far more common than alignment, they feel much more obliged and interested in being more communicative. There's no magic to checking alignment; it really is as simple as doing more talking. By that, we don't mean just increasing the number of words you use. We mean making the effort to check with people, again and again and again as needed to stay aligned (hence the labeling of alignment as a "mundane" topic in this book). This can be as simple as revisiting a decision, goal, ground rule, etc., that your group has crafted. For example, periodically ask your team or work groups, "Do we still agree on _____?" or "Has anything changed to affect what we want to do? Is the guideline we established working for all of us?"

This linking of communication and alignment will probably not be surprising. People who tell us about painful struggles they've had with past teams and misunderstandings that led to poor outcomes—or at least that made the work much harder than it needed to be—almost always frame it as a communication problem.

The nature of the communication has to be appropriate as well. Later in this book, we'll talk about a cross-functional team that really struggled to get work done. The sub-teams very rarely communicated with each other, and when they did it was in VERY detailed status reports (the kind that make your eyes glaze over when you're just 2 pages into a 40-page document). Now, the sub-teams have established direct connections between their members and status reports are both MUCH shorter and timelier—something along the lines of a text that says "FYI—the shipment will be 3 days late." Brief, frequent communications like this has prevented innumerable headaches for this company. (For details, see chap. 11).

Staying aligned definitely falls into the mundane category . . . but it can spill over into the tricky arena if a misalignment goes unrecognized for a long period of time. The two sides of the product development team featured at the start of this book, for example, were so misaligned around the details of what the goal of "quality" really meant that they spent the better part of two years in conflict with each other. There was resentment on both sides, hard feelings pent up from perceived slights and outright insults. Nobody . . . and we do mean nobody . . . on either side wanted to get together to have a friendly "What do we have in common" chat. But the team leaders made it happen, and in doing so got the team united around much more specific goals and guidelines.

How Aligned Are Your Teams?

Here's a test for you to try: Go to any regular meeting of a team you work with and ask everyone to write down the specific purpose or goal of the team. Then go around the room and have everyone read their statement out loud. The odds are good that you'll hear many different perceptions. Misalignment is all around you!

If you want to improve the performance of any group, start by ignoring the people who say that talking about alignment *again* is not necessary because, "We are already aligned." If you treat alignment as a one-and-done event, the odds are very high that your group will soon be out of alignment. The lesson is true not just around issues of where you're going (goals and purpose) but also how you're going to get there (ground rules, processes, roles, responsibilities, etc.).

—7—

Tricky 1 – Developing a Feedback Habit

And would some Power the small gift give us
To see ourselves as others see us!
It would from many a blunder free us . . .
—*Robert Burns, To a Louse [translation]*

Whenever we ask people how they feel about "feedback," the response is almost universally negative. To many people, this "f" word (feedback) conjures up images of being asked into someone's office to hear some criticism of work habits or attitudes. That is not the kind of feedback that we're championing.

We are focused on feedback that specifically relates to the *impact* of an individual's interaction behavior. This kind of feedback is necessary because, as the Burns quote demonstrates and we have mentioned before, people as a whole are notoriously poor at grasping the impact they have on a situation and how they may be contributing to any dysfunction they see.

One senior executive we knew, for example, had risen through the managerial ranks over a period of decades. Despite his apparent career success, we learned that others in the organization viewed him as a divisive, disruptive person. As a result, he had been shuffled around for years because nobody really wanted to work with him. The company didn't want to fire him, however, because he often made valuable contributions to the organization. Senior management knew the executive wasn't *trying* to be difficult. He just happened to be extremely action oriented: he became impatient in meetings, challenged the need to spend time on brainstorming and analysis, and constantly pushed people to make a call and move on. His impatience caused friction all around and made his departments less successful than they could have been . . . but he didn't know it.

This executive is not a singular example: all of us have some degree of self-ignorance. It could be around the negative impact of our behavior, as was the case with this executive, or around strengths we have that we don't value. To improve interaction, we have to address this incognizance and find ways to understand the kinds of impact we are having—both positive and negative—on others. The only way to do that is through feedback on our behavior: we need to hear directly from the people we affect how our way of interacting is either helping or hindering their effectiveness (and thus affecting our own).

The highly forceful executive in our example knew that others saw him as overbearing at times, but he viewed this behavior as a strength of his, a character trait that helped him get results. It wasn't until he heard descriptions of how his behavior made it harder for others to get their work done that he realized what he thought of as a positive was really a negative. People praised his ability to drive results, but said they'd realized it was usually safer to say nothing about potential problems and avoid raising alternative ideas rather than risk being on the receiving end of his impatience and antagonism. That gave him the motivation to change.

Few people find feedback "fun" and there is nothing particularly mundane about exposing oneself to criticism (and many people are uncomfortable receiving even *positive* feedback), which is why this chapter falls under the "tricky" category of interaction essentials. In fact, of all the techniques we talk about in this book, creating a norm around interaction feedback is the one that often is the most challenging to implement, in part because of some large barriers that can derail feedback attempts. In this chapter, we'll talk first about the barriers that make it difficult to establish a feedback habit and then describe steps you can take to overcome those barriers.

The Barriers to Feedback

Most people's intuition is that receiving feedback is harder than giving feedback, but we want to challenge that notion. When you are receiving feedback, you may be uncomfortable but you are in control. You have three options:

1) Accept the feedback.

2) Reject the feedback.

3) Do more checking to see if the feedback is validated by others.

The person giving the feedback also faces three options, but much less palatable ones! The feedback giver can:

- Give you honest feedback and risk having you become defensive (in effect punishing them for telling you something you don't want to hear).

- Lie to you and risk getting criticized for not being honest and open.

- Hold their tongue and run the same risks (accused of not being honest and open).

Because of the uncertainty about the receiver's reaction, feedback givers are often under stress—and the uncertainty and stress will be even greater if they think the person is very likely to react defensively. Let's face it: people don't get defensive if they are being complimented. That means defensiveness arises in situations where someone is listening to something they don't want to hear. Most of us, for example, would be very uncertain about telling someone who thinks of themselves as very *collaborative* that we thought they were more often *controlling*.

As we've discussed several times, defensive reactions are major obstacles to interaction because they discourage openness. People are unlikely to voluntarily give feedback to someone they know is defensive, and will be cautious and less than candid if the defensive person requests feedback. Also, preventing defensiveness is difficult because it is an emotional response spurred by many factors.

Therefore, when you are the receiver of feedback, you need to take special note of your reactions, especially if you see the feedback as a criticism. What is your typical reaction to negative feedback? Do you feel your anger rising? Do your emotional reactions get translated into subconscious gestures or other physiological reactions? Do you grimace? Avoid eye contact?

Catching the telltale signals of one's own defensiveness is a skill that can be learned and is invaluable in making others comfortable in giving you feedback. Remember, up to 90% of communication is non-verbal; people will pick up on your defensiveness regardless of what your words are saying. You don't want to send signals that tell the other person you're not interested in or don't want to hear what they have to say. This is true even if you think the person giving feedback is wrong or you take offense at the way they deliver the feedback. Almost always there is something to learn, even if it's badly "packaged" because the giver is venting or unskilled in delivering feedback. Typically there's a kernel of truth in almost all of the feedback you receive.

If you notice a defensive reaction, challenge yourself by asking questions, "Why don't I want to hear this? Why am I being resistant to learning?" We are often the most defensive about areas where we feel the most vulnerable, and perhaps where we need to do the most work.

To help train yourself to avoid having a defensive reaction that cuts off feedback, we recommend using the "*and* not *but*" rule. We hear conversations all the time where one person is giving constructive feedback to another person and that other person's first reaction is something like, "I can see why you feel that way, **BUT** on that occasion . . . [insert excuse]." The slightest intimation that you are in any way defensive (the "but" response) sends a message that you don't want to hear the feedback, cutting off the likelihood of any feedback in the future.

A much better response is to say, "I hear what you're saying . . . **AND** can you give me an example of that?" (Ask the same question of anyone else participating in the meeting.) Asking for examples gives you more information to work with and you can make a more informed judgment about whether you agree with the feedback or not. Often it opens up the conversation to much greater learning. In a discussion on this topic with an individual that we hold in high esteem, he explained his perspective on this idea as follows: "You get two kinds of people, those who learn and those who make excuses."

You can't fight defensiveness—your own or others'—with logic alone. What you *can* do is work to create an environment where defensiveness is low and learn to expect some element of emotion in people's reactions. The stress and emotional exposure surrounding interaction feedback makes it hard for people to enthusiastically embrace it right off the bat. For that reason, we recommend a three-step process for developing the feedback habit.

Step 1: Group Feedback on Group Processes

One of the best strategies for developing a norm around feedback is to start with **group-feedback-on-group-behavior** discussions. Periodically, have your work group or team discuss what it is doing well as a whole and what it needs to work on.

The idea is to get people comfortable with the concept that everything is open to improvement, and that feedback is one way to help identify what needs to be improved or preserved. Obviously, this isn't feedback on individual behaviors, but it helps develop a norm around improvement and feedback in the group. Having a group habit of talking about improvement ideas makes it easier to transition later on to providing individual feedback.

In these group-focused discussions, your team should also look at the impact of your group norms—do they create an environment that welcomes or that inhibits learning and feedback? Is there a lot of defensiveness on the team? (See sidebar.)

Un-discussables: The defensiveness index

One of the easiest ways for us to tell whether defensiveness is a problem on a team is to ask people if there are issues they simply never talk about—the "un-discussables." When we see groups with many un-discussables, we know that people have learned to NOT talk about some issues because of the reactions doing so elicited in the past.

Groups where people don't feel free to speak up about challenging issues are groups that will never fully close their interaction gaps. One executive we know latched onto this idea and added a new question that he asked at the end of his staff's weekly meeting: "Are we developing any un-discussables?" He says this tactic has become a non-threatening way that has helped his team become comfortable dealing with sensitive issues.

Step 2: Interaction Feedback in a Group Setting

In traditional techniques, people are encouraged to deliver feedback one-on-one. But that approach creates stress, especially if those delivering and receiving the feedback aren't skilled in knowing when and how to give feedback or how to receive it in a way that won't discourage further feedback. Until feedback becomes a group norm there is the risk that people will try it once or twice, find it challenging, and then withdraw into their comfort zones.

Imagine, for example, that a courageous employee walked into his boss's office one day and said, "You've really got to control your temper." How do you think the boss would react? Perhaps she could have held herself in check and *not* reacted, but it's highly likely that she would have felt resentful and defensive. Providing feedback that way is almost guaranteed to exacerbate the emotional component of interaction, which shuts down listening and learning.

To make it easier for people to develop the ability to provide feedback to others and listen to feedback themselves, we advise teams to experience personal feedback first in a group setting. Here's an example:

> We were helping a CEO and the leadership team of a very large building products manufacturer work on their productiveness as a team. In the morning session of one meeting, several of the executives were vocal in their frustration at the lack of feedback up and down the organization.
>
> So we proposed that they do some interaction feedback then and there. After some initial resistance, the CEO stepped up to the plate: "Well, I'd like to go ahead with it," he said. We then led a process where one executive would describe the collaborative strengths he or she thought they brought to the team and also behaviors they thought may be impeding the team in some way. For example, one executive stated that she tended to over-analyze data. Another said he got impatient when people avoided taking action.

> *After each person spoke up, the team would discuss whether they agreed with the person's self-perception, and then offer their own comments about how the person could improve their performance as a fellow team member.*
>
> *As a result of the discussion, most of these executives had some form of personal "aha": perhaps realizing that the team valued a strength they brought to the team (opening the garage door on the parked Ferrari), discovering that something they thought was a problem was in fact not an issue for others, or uncovering practical steps they could take to address their weak spots. Everyone came away with ideas on how they personally could improve.*

At the end of the day, the team agreed that they'd had a very productive session with open and meaningful discussions unlike previous interactions in the team. This session initiated a new pattern of continuous learning by the leadership team. Everyone readily agreed to a follow-up session six months later so they could track their progress and identify steps for further improvement.

As you can see, the purpose of interaction feedback is not to make everyone perfect. It is simply to learn how to interact and work more effectively as a team. To achieve that goal, here are some basic ground rules that we have found helpful:

- **Everyone participates.** As we've talked about before, any individual experience that is not shared by a group is a sure-fire recipe for a way to *not* change a group norm. You need to create a shared experience within the group if you want to change the norm. Also, if everyone has gone through the same experience, no one will feel picked on or singled out. This creates a sense of fairness all around. Lastly, equal participation means everyone was involved in both giving and receiving feedback, which helps to build their skills.

- **The feedback should represent a balance between how to better leverage someone's strengths and how to better manage their weaknesses.** The goal is for everyone to recognize that they bring a combination of strengths and weaknesses to the team. That way, any weaknesses or negative impacts of someone's behavior are treated in the context of the positive contributions that the person makes to the group. Without this balance, people may become defensive and begin to feel as if they're being targeted, even though that is never the intent.

The leadership team in our example quickly gravitated to suggestions on how the team could best use the strengths that each individual brought to the team and what strategies the team could use to make sure that any gaps or issues were properly addressed. Framing the purpose of the session in this way plays a critical role in developing group ownership over interaction effectiveness.

- **The feedback cannot be open-ended; it must be about the impact of someone's behavior.** Any comments shared in this kind of exercise have to be focused around how someone's behavior affects the ability of others to interact with that person and with each other. When the goal is to improve interaction, it's okay to say to someone, "When you cut me off in the meeting, I didn't have a chance to finish my thought." That kind of statement provides data that links a specific behavior to the consequence of that behavior: the person did X and Y happened. The person then has a chance to think about the input and decide what to do with it.

In contrast, it's not OK to say, "You really ruined the meeting. Why don't you let others talk sometimes!" With that kind of statement, all people hear is a critical judgment, a personal attack—which is likely to elicit an emotional, defensive reaction.

- **Have an expert facilitator leading the exercise.** It's just common sense to use a seasoned facilitator in a sensitive situation like this where everyone is practicing complicated new skills and being placed in situations that can easily bog down (because of natural defensiveness, perhaps). Using an expert facilitator gives people a chance to apply theories about feedback to a real-life experience. That helps build new skills. Plus, the facilitator will help keep people focused on the goal of improvement and encourage non-defensive behavior.

Having an expert facilitator on hand helps the team create a safe environment that supports openness and builds trust. This approach creates an atmosphere that allows the feedback to be delivered in a way that people can really hear it and process it.

Step 3: Develop 1-on-1 Feedback Skills

Once the team has become more comfortable with group feedback, people can start trying out 1-on-1 feedback with others in the team. Eventually, 1-on-1 feedback becomes the norm for most groups we work with.

The same ground rules about keeping the feedback focused on impact apply, as well as any feedback techniques that most people have learned. That includes being careful about the timing. In teams where feedback has become an embedded norm, providing real-time feedback in a team setting is fine. Teams that can operate this way move through issues much faster than those in which members are walking on eggshells around each other. But for practical purposes, it is advisable to deliver most feedback in private.

Using Disclosure To Encourage Feedback

No matter what your position is on a team, you can shift the feedback dynamics in a positive direction if you develop the skill of inviting feedback in a way that lowers the other person's concerns about how you are going to react. (We'll talk more about the special impact of leaders' attitudes towards interaction feedback in Chapter 9.)

The way to do this is to start with **disclosure**: describe to another person (colleague, team member, direct report) a specific skill or behavior that you want feedback on and ask for their input. This technique is straightforward, and it starts with you having a personal goal around improving your interaction skills. Here are a few quick examples:

Charles's team had decided to focus on improving the use of their meeting time. Their meetings often ran long and the estimated times for agenda items were way off. Based on feedback he'd received in a group setting, Charles realized he was a big part of the problem because he tended to ramble on about his favorite topics.

He acknowledged that reality at the start of a meeting and asked his colleagues to call him on it if he was straying off topic or simply taking too long to make his point. They were happy to oblige!

Besides learning to recognize when he was droning on, Charles took steps to become more succinct. For example, he'd print out copies of the agendas ahead of time and jot down notes on key points he wanted to make, then speak to those points when the time came.

#

Donna had a natural talent around coordinating work, and she wanted to make sure that all of her team's tasks were clearly assigned. But she'd received feedback that some people saw her as manipulative, which created some friction on the team.

So she asked Dave, the team leader, to help her out. "Dave," she said, "could you observe me at the next team meeting and let me know if I'm doing anything that you think is manipulative?" Dave agreed, and after the next team meeting, they met one-on-one again.

Dave shared two observations with her. First, he said that she sometimes went over-the-top in terms of flattering people whom she wanted to take on a particular task. "You said something to Emanuel about how he was the best data guy in the company and you just knew he'd want to take the lead on the analysis we're about to do," said Dave. "I believe you think that, but you brought up the point several times, so it started to sound insincere. It's nice that you appreciate the talents of other people on the team, but don't go overboard."

"Second," Dave continued, "several times you went around the room asking everyone's opinion on an issue. At the outset we thought we were all contributing to a solution. But as the discussion went on, it seemed like you had already made up your mind before engaging the rest of the team. So it felt like asking for input was just a manipulation to get us to agree with you. If you have already made up your mind or are leaning strongly in one direction, it would be much better if you put your cards on the table at the outset then asked people for their ideas."

Donna took these lessons to heart and worked to change her behavior. She also periodically asked Dave (in private) to comment on whether she was coming across as more collaborative than manipulative.

At one level, these examples sound very simple. But the fact that a person is asking others for feedback accomplishes several important interaction goals:

- It demonstrates the person's openness to learning.

- It demonstrates their personal commitment to supporting the group norm that improving interaction is important.

- It helps to build trust.

- It can bring an un-discussable issue out into the open and make it discussable.

Also, inviting feedback gives you, the feedback receiver, much more control over the situation. You decide when it happens and who is involved by virtue of choosing the moment to ask a specific person for their input. You also decide *what* is discussed because you name the topic that concerns you and *how much* information is shared. In the first mini-case above, Charles involved his team in helping to improve an issue that was a priority for the whole team (better use of meeting time). In the second story, Donna got advice from a selected colleague on how to correct an issue that was making her less effective on the team.

Disclosure has another important role to play in effective interaction: it is an excellent approach for breaking the ice with someone after an uncomfortable exchange (unconstructive conflict and/or an interaction that raised negative emotions). Typically what happens when there has been an angry or awkward exchange is those involved pretend it never happened. This mini "un-discussable," which everyone clearly remembers, can create a permanent dent in the trust in the team. Team members may tend to walk on eggshells around each other and some may emotionally withdraw and not fully engage with the other people afterwards.

The next time you observe or participate in poor interaction, try to engage the person or people after the event by disclosing how you felt you contributed to the negativity that occurred. Try something along the lines of "I think I could have stated my opinions more clearly" or "I think I let my emotions get out of hand." This disarms the other person and almost always starts a two-way dialogue in which they will offer their views on how *they* may have contributed to the negative dynamics in the discussion. Together, you can then talk about ways in which you can take responsibility—individually and collectively—for avoiding a similar situation in the future.

Learning to Love This "F" Word

Tim was a young, ambitious junior executive at a technology company. He felt he was smart enough to make decisions on his own and also believed it was his job as a leader to make decisions to pass on to his staff. (He thought of himself as decisive; his staff thought of him as dictatorial.)

Tim's natural tendency to focus on business deadlines was exacerbated by working in a new company: the pressure to produce results was so strong that he had no patience for what he considered "idle chatter" on the job. However, he took non-talking to an extreme, seldom discussing anything of personal interest to himself and not even talking about the business issues with his team or with anyone else in the company.

Senior executives weren't aware that Tim was poor at interaction—all they knew was that Tim's department was not functioning well and there were serious collaboration issues between his department and other departments. They could see that other groups ended up duplicating work because they didn't know that Tim's team had already done it.

Developing state-of-the-art technology needs a highly collaborative environment, but the people in Tim's department were operating in survival mode. They didn't have the energy to worry about what was going on in other departments; they just wanted to keep their jobs, and keeping silent seemed to be the best option. (Though frankly, they wasted a lot of time *complaining to each other about Tim and how hard it was to work in the department!)*

If Tim had a window into his interaction skills, it was shut tight and boarded over. He was a very private person and kept himself isolated from his work group and the rest of the company. There was a great deal he did not share about his thinking and reasoning, so others knew little about why he behaved the way he did. Also, he simply never gave a second thought to the impact of his behavior on others; doing so wasn't part of his makeup. As a result, he never had the opportunity to learn about why he wasn't getting the results he wanted.

Few of us are as isolated from others as Tim was, but he is a perfect illustration of why people who are closed off from input from co-workers and never share anything about themselves are going to have a difficult time improving interaction. Tim's co-workers could never learn how to interact better with him because he never told them how their behavior affected him (he avoided *giving* feedback), plus he never wanted to hear about how he was standing in the way of interaction (he avoided *receiving* feedback).

Though "feedback" has negative connotations for many people, most learn to view this particular "f" word quite differently after they have learned about the absolute necessity of feedback for improving interaction. They don't want to be isolated like Tim and closed off from learning. After having a chance to both give and receive interaction feedback, people see that it helps them become more effective at accomplishing their own tasks more quickly, playing to their strengths more easily, removing friction from relationships with co-workers, and so on.

One last point: Over the past decade and more, the business world has been abuzz with talk of "employee empowerment." One ingredient that has been missing in many of the resulting efforts has been the empowerment that comes from having better self-awareness. Having the opportunity to use feedback to improve their effectiveness provides a direct WIIFM for people, an incentive for them to participate in interaction improvement.

Getting feedback on the impact of their behavior gives people important insights that help them perform better on the job and chart a professional development path that can build on and expand their strengths. Every person profiled in this chapter gained knowledge about themselves that they could use to become more effective, not just in the setting where the feedback occurred but in all interactions they have on the job (and even in their private lives). If that's not empowerment, what is?

—8—

Tricky 2 –
Constructive Use of Conflict

Conflict is a curious thing. It has both a positive side and a negative side, depending on how it is dealt with.

Where there are large interaction gaps, conflict can rapidly degenerate into the destructive variety that will severely limit what a group can achieve. At best, destructive conflict raises barriers that cause rework and delays; at worst, it will stop collaboration in its tracks and make existing interaction gaps larger. That happens when the conflict erupts into an all-out war between people with different ideas, perspectives, or beliefs. The combatants retreat into their corners, not really interested in hearing more from their opponents. Thoughts, ideas, and opinions are squelched because no one wants to reignite tempers. The people or groups work *around* issues rather than resolving them. Accusatory emails get sent up the hierarchy, both sides blaming the other for problems. Progress is reduced to a crawl, creativity is stifled, and hard feelings carry over into everything these people and groups do. This kind of destructive conflict is a common reason why groups or teams fail to achieve their goals.

Yet constructive, energizing conflict is absolutely essential if your group wants to get the best results possible. This kind of conflict helps teams push the boundaries of creativity. After all, if there were no differences of opinion between the people in your group, then why are you all working together in the first place? The only times we've seen a group with no disagreements is when people were too scared or intimidated to say what they were really thinking. That is just as deadly for effective interaction as hot-tempered arguments.

With constructive conflict, people argue passionately about ideas or goals or decisions with the aim of getting the best result. The attitude that underpins healthy arguments is not who's right or wrong, but rather what's right for the team or organization. Somehow, some way, the team finds a common solution that is better than anything the players would have come up with on their own.

The positive side of conflict is why you should not try to avoid it altogether. But to ensure your group does not get derailed by its destructive side, you will need to deal with conflict openly. Keeping conflict on the constructive path is one of the most critical skills that any group can develop.

Covering all the aspects of conflict is beyond the scope of this book. Here, we're focusing on how you can avoid and manage conflict to some degree by treating it as an integral part of interaction. We will contrast destructive and constructive conflict and highlight the many ways in which destructive conflict undermines effective interaction. We'll then discuss what to do to minimize the chances for destructive conflict and maximize the odds of using conflict as a powerful force for improved performance. We'll also talk about what to do when emotions cross the line—when the conflict is generating more heat than light— because it's bound to happen to even the best of teams.

A Broad Interpretation of Conflict

In reality, most people make a distinction between simple arguments and true conflict. But the principles for getting past differences, whether large or small, are the same. So in this chapter, we will consider a "conflict" as any situation where people have a disagreement.

The Bad and Ugly, and The Good

There are five people on the engineering leadership team for a consumer packaging company. The group's purpose is to establish the strategic direction and priorities for the department and manage the day-to-day operations of the engineering group. Bruce is the department head. He is very experienced and knowledgeable, and has been with the company almost from its inception. He is well-respected but people know that he gets touchy and defensive under pressure. Evelyn is a senior manager and Bruce's second-in-command. The three other managers on the team represent engineering, logistics, and quality control.

Before we describe one particular incident that is characteristic of how conflict is handled on this team, here is some background: Bruce has been effective in the past because he has a laser focus on getting the job done. When an issue arises, he will often go directly to the people in the various departments rather than deal with the three managers who are on his leadership team. These managers greatly resent having Bruce go behind their backs, but since he's the boss, they don't want to speak up. There is a simmering resentment that has created a dynamic where the managers are more interested in protecting their own interests than in doing what's best for the team. They don't turn to Evelyn because she is known to lose her cool unexpectedly and become emotional over matters trivial and large.

Here's what happened that pushed this team over a conflict cliff:

At one point, Bruce and Evelyn were at loggerheads over a major decision. They'd been arguing about it for weeks, but neither budged. One of the other managers had a novel idea for resolving the differences, but didn't raise it because he thought that Bruce or Evelyn would just shut him down.

When it came time for a vote, Evelyn thought she had the support of the other three managers, but all three of them voted with Bruce instead. She became quite flustered, raised her voice, and spit out her words. Then she stormed out of the room. Everyone else sat silently; most were shaken.

Over the next few months, the blow-up was not brought up in the leadership meetings but the team never regained its previous productivity level (let alone improve). People were very reluctant to speak up, whether to ask questions or to raise new ideas. In fact, there was very little discussion. Evelyn and everyone else found it easier to simply go along with whatever Bruce recommended.

That's the bad and ugly type of conflict. As you can see—and may have experienced yourself—poorly handled conflict creates robotic groups where people minimize interaction of all kinds. Bad and ugly conflict can also create a vicious cycle by undermining trust in a group, which makes it more likely that destructive conflict will arise again, and if handled badly will further erode trust, and on and on.

As we hope to have convinced you by now, teams never do their best if some people don't speak up, if competing ideas aren't considered and discussed, or if positional power is allowed to dominate over knowledge and insight. But that's exactly what happens when destructive conflict is allowed to interfere with effective interaction.

There's another fact about destructive conflict that was evident here: its impact usually trickles out in all directions to affect others. In Bruce and Evelyn's case, the inability of these two senior managers to collaborate led to chasms throughout the engineering department. Anyone else in the company who needed engineering advice usually had to go to three or four people because they were never sure they were getting a complete answer. Duplication of effort became rampant in many areas. Well-meaning managers became paralyzed because of clear contradictions in the directions that the bosses were giving them.

Constructive conflict

Now let's contrast the picture of that company with an example of conflict handled correctly. Katherine was the brand new CEO of a training and development company. She was logical, measured, and analytical in her approach to problem solving. Her COO was very creative and impulsive. Though they came at problems from very different perspectives, Katherine knew how to use those differences to help her team be more effective.

For example, the COO, who was called the "walking idea engine," would often come up with big picture ideas. Some were very sound; others were totally impractical. Rather than shut down his creativity because she knew some of the ideas wouldn't work, Katherine made sure that the whole team got to offer opinions about the COO's ideas. To draw out the quieter members and restrain those who were fond of consuming airtime, she'd make sure to solicit the opinions of the rest of the team. She would also challenge the COO to think more about the practicality of his ideas.

Everybody on the executive team got the same treatment. If anyone raised a new idea—even a wild and crazy one—Katherine would make sure the idea was not lost. The ensuing discussions were highly valued by the team and would often lead to insights even if the original ideas weren't used. If people became judgmental in their statements or drifted into criticizing people personally rather than sticking to discussing the merits of the ideas, Katherine would steer the conversation back into a more productive direction.

Most importantly, conflict was dealt with openly. When discussions became heated or when she sensed some people shutting down, Katherine would point out the issue and use her judgment about whether to address it right in the meeting or wait until afterwards.

Gradually, the team grew in confidence and its performance improved. The team took less time to come to conclusions, and came up with new ideas that drove the company ahead, including ideas for capitalizing on market trends with new products. There was more accountability because the executives were more open and honest with each other. The more they accomplished, the more energized the team became.

The Best Preventive: Trust

Although trust is a word that is often overused or misused, the concept of trust is unavoidable when your goal is to lessen destructive conflict. Think about the two examples we just went through or about times when you've been in conflict with others. What made the difference between situations where conflict was a roadblock and where conflict was an asset? The answer, to a large extent, is trust or the lack of it.

In the second case study, Katherine did a great job of building trust on her team. She was consistent in her reactions and always responded to new ideas by encouraging people to speak up. The more she did this, the more the people on her team felt comfortable expressing their ideas, even if—or, rather, *especially when*—they didn't agree with others on the team. When the arguments got heated, which they sometimes did, Katherine enforced standards of courtesy and respect, no matter what the topic. Everyone soon realized that the norm on this team was that if someone disagreed with or didn't understand someone else's position, their role was to ask questions until they did understand, not to continue trying to explain their own position. They knew that both inside *and outside* the meeting rooms, they were a true team and everyone had each other's backs.

By contrast, in the first case study with Bruce and Evelyn, there was little trust within the management team. The managers interpreted

Bruce's tendency to work around them and go directly to their staff as going behind their backs, and they didn't trust him to treat them as equals. They didn't trust Evelyn because of her unpredictable temper and her extreme reactions. Since they did not trust their leaders, the choices they most often made were to keep their opinions to themselves. When people do not trust each other, they are likely to take any criticism or disagreement on a very personal level . . . and once an argument becomes personal, it's quite easy for the conflict to become destructive. This kind of toxic mix on the management team shackled their ability to get work done because people were keeping their creativity, ideas, perspectives, and knowledge to themselves.

Trust is not something you can work on directly. It is a predictable outcome when supportive patterns of behavior are maintained over weeks, months, and years. However, there are active steps you can take

---

Understanding the Source and Destination

Whenever you're dealing with conflict, it helps to first sort out two issues: the basis of the conflict and what you want to achieve. That will help you determine how to approach resolving the differences and whether you might need help doing so.

In general, dealing with conflict that is based on values is very tricky and resolution may not be possible. Where the conflict is mainly emotional, skillful handling of an individual or group can defuse the situation, which may include allowing people to vent in a controlled and safe manner (a valuable but underused strategy).

Also, the best possible outcome of conflict is finding a true win-win solution. Ideally, no one should feel like a loser (or even a winner if it means someone else lost).

As our own team trials have shown, when you are part of a group or groups that have a common goal, the best outcome is achieved only when people are open to seeing an issue through many viewpoints not just their own. Groups do best when they come to a mutual understanding of an agreement on what the best answer is, given all the information and limitations of a situation. This is the mindset that leads to win-win solutions.

to create an environment that fosters trust and minimizes the chances that disagreements will turn into destructive conflict, as we'll discuss next.

Making Differences an Asset:
The Secrets to Constructive Conflict

In Chapter 5, we talked about the need to do some tedious and unexciting work to establish a foundation of good interaction. Mundane practices such as using agendas, establishing discussion ground rules, using both advocacy and inquiry, etc., are behaviors that reflect underlying values of respect between team members. Positive team norms created around listening to each other, having sound meetings, being clear about the purpose of discussions, and so on, can go a long way towards keeping discussions productive and focused on the team's purpose.

Beyond those basics, there are a number of steps you can take to maximize the chance that conflict will be constructive—meaning it will help you achieve a win-win solution focused on needs without getting sidetracked by destructive conflict.

1. Understand the dynamics of discussions

If you observe the discussion of a high-performing team, what you'll witness is that a great deal of useful information comes to light. The high-quality dialogue very frequently leads to a decision that turns out to be the best choice in the long run. The norms that lead to good discussions are based on the following insights:

- Most discussions have a **divergent phase** (where thinking broadly is an asset) and a **convergent phase** (where the group reaches a decision and moves forward). At the outset get your group to agree on whether it's time for divergent or convergent thinking. Making this distinction can be very helpful in getting group members to see the value of different styles and avoid the conflict that comes when people get impatient with a type of discussion that doesn't come naturally to them.

- During a divergent discussion, the goal is to generate ideas not narrow down options or reach conclusions. Therefore, enforce ground rules aimed at making sure that everyone's ideas are shared with the whole team and that analysis or criticism is suspended. Do not allow people with more forceful personalities or roles to overshadow those who are more reserved. Most especially, make sure that the off-the-wall or unusual ideas are heard. Hearing a minority opinion is often critical to reaching new insights.

- During convergent discussions, use the skills of the people who are best at synthesizing ideas, analyzing the options, or coming up with practical solutions.

- If you anticipate a particular kind of conflict, include someone in the discussion who can bring an impartial point of view.

- If any special interests or viewpoints are slowing the team down, find another way to deal with them—for example, have the people who love planning get together offline to draft plans they can share with the team during a meeting (with the caveat that they remain open to suggestions).

2. Put Team Role strengths to good use

Teams with an insight into their Team Role composition function better than those that lack this awareness because they can use their talents more effectively. For example:

- The Team Worker skills represent people who are naturally attuned to things like tone of voice and gestures. People with this talent are very adept at detecting when tension and behavior is creeping into a dialogue, and can be relied on to point that out to the team if allowed (or invited) to do so. They are often less invested in the issue or issues that are driving any escalation to unconstructive conflict, and can help the team to maintain its norm of embracing conflict as a source of creativity.

- People strong in the Monitor Evaluator role are naturally very reasoned and analytical. Draw on their strengths if you find your group falling into discussions that are not well-supported by facts or logic. These people can help your team decide what information could help you make a better-informed decision.

3. Anticipate and plan for barriers

One of the best ways to avoid destructive conflict is to anticipate issues or ideas that are likely to trigger strong differences of opinion or perspective, and then come up with a plan of attack ahead of time. Here's one example:

> A junior executive once had a major confrontation with his boss over an issue of how to get a particular job done. He was subsequently transferred to a different division. Several years later, the two found themselves working together once again, though the once-junior executive was now of equal rank.

To avoid repeating their past interaction, the two estab-lished a set of agreements (aka ground rules). They defined areas where their approaches or viewpoints were so different that agreement was unlikely. Fortunately, their areas of strong feelings did not overlap much—that meant each could defer decisions in that area to the other, thereby avoiding the most likely sources of conflict.

They talked about areas where both would have equal input, and what that would look like. They even talked about behaviors each had employed in their prior interactions that had really bothered them, and agreed that they could call each other out if those behaviors surfaced again.

If they came to the verge of strong disagreements, often-times one of them would say something like, "Remember, we agreed that I'd have the final say here," or, "We agreed to handle this another way."

Because they dealt with the issue of their past differences openly, the two executives were able to charter a new relation-ship that allowed them to be much more productive this time around. Also, since they had established how to deal with a number of issues, they came to see that their differences could actually work to their advantage.

A second way to anticipate barriers goes back to the Team Role framework once again. As we talked about in Chapter 4, having a mix of roles is generally an asset for the team, but it does create potential conflicts. Sometimes the conflict is because two roles are very different in how they handle different tasks; sometimes because the strength or allowable weakness of a role creates the potential for problems (for example, two people with very strong Shaper roles may find the force of their personalities causes them to clash). Once you're aware of the potential clashes, your team should develop a plan for dealing with them should they occur. (Revisit the Carla and Duane story in Chapter 4 for an example of how this was done.)

Anticipating these kinds of barriers won't eliminate all the potential sources of conflict, but you'll have a much smoother ride (and shorter path to success) than if potential barriers become true roadblocks.

4. Have a "final decision maker" rule

While the advice in this chapter and other chapters will help you avoid some conflicts, almost all groups will eventually run into a situation where people simply will not agree on what is best. That's the kind of roadblock that no group or team can afford when it relates to a decision that it is responsible for making.

That's why we advise groups to explicitly agree on a set of ground rules around decision making, and have a back-up plan for times when they cannot reach agreement around a key decision or they encounter a conflict they are unable to resolve.

The first step is to agree on who will be the final decision maker. Usually, but not always, this is the team leader. The team then spells out the options the final decision maker has when the team faces an impasse. Here are three typical options, all of which are workable if not ideal:

1) If the decision maker feels they have the necessary understanding and information, they simply make the call themselves.

2) The decision maker can delegate their authority to someone they feel is in a better position to make the decision, such as someone with a particular expertise or base of experience. (With the understanding that the final decision maker will support the decision made by the other person.)

3) If time allows, the decision maker can push the decision back to the team for further discussions or to a subgroup that will be

charged with coming up with a recommendation for the team to consider.

The third option is valuable because it avoids two pitfalls: First, it takes some of the pressure off the final decision maker who may otherwise feel obliged to make a decision even if they lack key information. Second, it prevents a team that may be uncomfortable with conflict from taking the easy path of continually pushing decisions up to the leader.

The final ground rule is that once the decision is made, everyone on the team will actively support that decision even if it wasn't the one they originally wanted.

Agreeing on ground rules—and documenting them—ahead of time is an essential and excellent way of preventing conflict from becoming personal. If a situation gets heated, people can diffuse the emotional reactions by referring to agreed-on ground rules: "Remember, we all agreed that Seth could make the call in these situations."

How to Recover from a Blow Up

Whenever we ask people to define "conflict," they speak about people or groups who have different ideas or priorities. They focus on the rational side of disagreement. However, the hardest conflict to deal with is when the emotional side takes over. There are situations where a group or team can have an unexpected blow up. It happens even in the best of groups. (Sometimes, the cause is not even related to a work issue— perhaps someone is simply having a bad day, is facing a health crisis, or going through a divorce or other major stress. Which means there is nothing happening in the meeting *per se* that caused the blow up.)

To achieve high levels of interaction effectiveness, you have to deal head on with a blow up; the worst thing you can do when conflict goes awry is to ignore the issue. If you do not address conflict at the outset, it will only continue down the destructive path and get worse over time, as illustrated by the Bruce & Evelyn story on page 127. Your group or organization will suffer if you do, paying the price in terms of wasted effort, stalemate, duplication, and so on. If, in subsequent meetings, there is a pretense that the blow up did not occur, it is likely to become an "un-discussable" and create permanent damage to the trust levels and fabric of the team.

As obvious as the following steps sound, to deal with a blow up we suggest first going back to the basics before trying anything more complicated.

Basic 1: Do not to try to deal with it in the moment

Basic physiology teaches us that when strong emotions take over, our rational thinking, our ability to listen and to feel empathy are largely shut down. Yet those are the very skills needed to resolve a conflict. So step back, have the people involved in the conflict take as much time as they need to calm down.

We were working with a negotiation team that put this idea to great use. Off-and-on, they had to spend months in the same room with representatives of their company's union. We all know that such negotiations can be fraught with tension and have a strong emotional component.

Originally, the negotiation team would meet every evening to debrief the day. However, after several discussions simply led to disagreements, the team established a "Go easy on ourselves" mantra (and its associated "sleep on it" rule). They no longer tried to discuss issues when they were tired and stressed at the end of the day. The first time they tried this, a person involved in a strong argument one afternoon came back the next morning and admitted that after thinking about it overnight, he realized he agreed with the ideas he'd been arguing against the previous day!

The amount of time needed to calm down will vary by situation and individual, and we can't provide any hard-and-fast rule. Essentially, you'll have to use your judgment. If your group is new to dealing with strong conflict, it's likely people will need to sleep on the issues overnight or even take a few days to reflect on what happened. More experienced people may just need to count to ten or take a coffee break to reach a calmer state where they can discuss what just happened.

Basic 2: Never say in an email what you should say on the phone (and never say on the phone what you should say in person)

We have never seen a conflict that was resolved by email. Have you? A conflict that has blown up by definition has a big emotional component. It's nearly impossible to interpret emotions in an email and very hard to do over the phone. So stick to face-to-face meetings after some time has passed. Using the less-direct approach of an email or call can be a way of sidestepping the issue. It takes a certain amount of courage to have frank discussions on sensitive matters.

Basic 3: Apologize

If you were in the wrong—for the way you acted if not in the ideas you were supporting—say so. Yes, we know that many people find apologizing very difficult, but it is a skill that people interested in effective interaction must master. Even if you think the other person or group was 90% in the wrong and you share just 10% of the blame, acknowledge that you did something that made the conflict worse.

Basic 4: Involve a neutral third party

When people or groups are involved in a blow up or have long-standing resentments, it may be impossible for them to deal with the issues objectively. That's why we recommend they bring in a neutral third party—someone not on the team and not involved in the contentious issue—to help them move past the conflict. In some cases, having a neutral party involved is enough to break the ice and allow the people or groups to calmly discuss what happened and come to a resolution.

Getting Past Strong Conflict:
Leaving the Past Behind

There is a basic principle in all conflict resolution (not just when strong conflict is involved) that trying to figure out who was right or wrong in the past is a waste of time. That's why the immediate goal when dealing with strong conflict is NOT for the parties to resolve their differences. The more realistic goal is simply for both sides to better understand what happened in the past and get some insights about the other side's perspectives.

One of our favorite methods for getting groups back on track and accomplishing the goal of understanding without actually resolving past conflict is called "mirror imaging." Going into the details of mirror imaging is beyond the scope of this book, but essentially the two people or groups identify their most highly contentious issues. For each issue, the groups describe their perception of how they currently interact with each other around that issue, focusing on four categories (Figure 17):

- How they perceive themselves

- How they perceive the other group

- How they think the other group perceives themselves

- How they think the other group perceives them

In each category, the group must provide examples that illustrate how their perceptions were formed.

Figure 17: The Mirror Imaging Structure

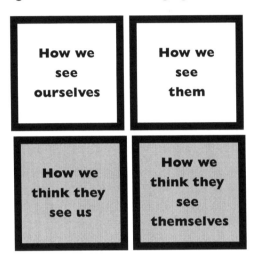

The groups come together and share their perspectives on one issue using a highly structured procedure guided by an expert facilitator (there are no open discussions, each group speaks through an appointed spokesperson). They repeat the process for the second issue, and then a third if necessary. By the time the parties get through the second or third issue, they realize that the underlying cause of the contention is almost always a lack of trust or a lack of communication. The facilitator then helps them revisit each issue and negotiate how they will work together around that issue and move forward in ways that reflect greater trust and more open communication.

What's critical about the mirror imaging method is that there is no attempt to resolve or forget anything that has happened in the past. You will never get people to agree on exactly who said what, or who was responsible for what. However, clearing up misconceptions and getting the parties to create a shared view of the future has proven to be an extremely effective way of helping them move beyond a history of poor interaction.

Conclusion

Groups come together because they need different skills, knowledge, and perspectives to solve problems or even just to perform everyday work. It is in their differences that people discover greater creativity and innovation. But there is a tipping point where disagreement can devolve into unconstructive conflict, where emotions and defensiveness prevent constructive discussions and progress. That's why learning to get the good from conflict and avoid the bad is one of the trickiest aspects of interaction.

There's no team leader and no team that gets it right all the time. Our best advice is to acknowledge that strong conflicts will arise. Be proactive in doing as much as you can to prevent the factors that push conflict towards the path of destruction; be open to learning how to hit that goal more often. If conflict gets destructive, go back to the basics of respect and civility, and follow the rule set by the negotiation team we discussed earlier: be kind to yourself. That's really the best that any of us can do.

From Novelty to Routine

Creating the norms and shared language
of effective interaction

The subjects covered in this part of the book describe steps you can take to create new norms and new expectations around effective interaction. As you begin working on these techniques, people will begin using a shared language that helps them communicate more clearly about difficult issues and find ways to work with others more effectively. People in your meetings will start asking "who is doing the 3Ps for the next meeting?" to make sure they know why the meeting is necessary, what the outcome should be, and how they could contribute to that outcome. Groups will want to do a Team Map so they will know how to use the skills within their groups to maximum effect. Individuals may begin asking you for interaction feedback so they can constantly improve.

To help you move from the point where these concepts are interesting novelties to where they are truly engrained norms that have become routine, we have four suggestions for getting started:

1. Give People a Reason to Care

Norms of group behavior cannot be imposed from the outside. It's the people inside the group who shape the norm, and they are not going to change or develop new norms if they don't see a good reason for doing so.

When dealing with behavioral changes, lecturing people about the need for the change will have no impact on its own. What WILL have an impact is creating an experience where people become educated about the norm and what it means, and get to practice the new norm and experience the benefits themselves. Once you've participated in effective meetings—where the purpose is clear, agenda items flow smoothly, time is well managed, and everyone's ideas get heard no matter how contentious the topic—you'll have a much harder time going back to the old ways. Once you've worked in a team where people are playing to their interaction strengths and where weaknesses are no longer an impediment, you'll start to get frustrated with groups who haven't been exposed to using Team Role theory. (The same is true for the other norms.)

Creating the conviction that working on interaction is important—a conviction that will be strong enough to overcome the tedious aspects of the work required—can only come from experiencing the benefits firsthand. We use the decision-making simulation described in Chapter 1; you should consider doing something similar so that people get a chance to learn and practice new skills under expert guidance.

2. Develop a Strategy Based on Team Role Composition

One of the tangible benefits of working with the Team Role model is being able to use that knowledge to develop strategies for being more effective. We've talked about several ideas already in the previous chapters. For example, shared knowledge of Team Role strengths and weaknesses can be used to help you assign team tasks, run more effective meetings, stay aligned, and even deal with conflict more effectively.

This knowledge should also influence your overall strategy. In our experience, the Team Role composition of a group makes a big difference in how quickly group members will be convinced to try "this interaction stuff," how quickly they will adopt new behaviors, and how easy it will be to sustain the changes. The "personality" of the team overall should influence your strategy. A team that predominantly has very analytical people, for example, may require a lot of convincing up front but generally shows strong support once the team commits to the new direction. In contrast, groups with many divergent, creative thinkers (who are typically weak on follow-through) may see enthusiastic support up front—so adoption of changes goes quickly—but may find it harder to sustain the changes over the long term.

Every effective leader knows they have to customize their approaches to best engage the people they are trying to lead. Information gained from the Team Role analysis gives you a framework for gaining deeper insights into the composition of your work groups or teams, and therefore an understanding of which approach will be most effective.

3. Use a Coach in the Early Stages

None of the techniques discussed in the recent chapters come naturally to people at first. So there will always be an awkward phase where people are trying to both implement the norms *and* complete the regular work of their group or team. It's very hard to juggle both considerations as long as both require a lot of attention. Plus, remember that the pull of the group is going to be towards its old norms.

That's why every team needs to have someone championing and policing the implementation of the new norms until they become engrained habits. This is true no matter what the personality of your team. There are simply too many challenges involved in creating new norms, factors that make your odds of success very low if the group tries to go it alone.

Our recommendation is that early on (during the first 3 to 6 months), plan on using a coach, typically someone from outside the team. Teams commonly use a manager from the next level up, an HR professional, or a process improvement expert who understands the principles of these norms and can monitor application of the changes and provide unbiased feedback. This coach can come from inside or outside the organization, just as long as they are trained in team dynamics and are effective observers. Their role will be:

- Helping the group define what norm(s) it wants to focus on.

- Guiding the group in developing methods that reflect that norm.

- Observing the group's behavior and whether it is consistent or inconsistent with the norm.

- Providing feedback to the group on what it did well and what could be done differently.

Eventually, the coach's role will fade away as the team becomes more competent at the new norms, and team members can self-monitor implementation.

4. Start Slow

The problem with changing norms is that it sounds much easier than it really is. Most of what we've talked about in the preceding chapters is conceptually simple, but as we discussed before, a fatal flaw is to underestimate how difficult it can be to accomplish the simple. Expect it to be hard to develop new habits. Here's what we recommend:

1) Use the Interaction Index[6] with your group to rate yourselves on how well you are doing in the five areas shown.

2) After that evaluation, PICK ONE area to work on. To do that, think about a project or critical issue that needs addressing and focus on developing a new norm that will help you work on that challenge. This just-in-time approach avoids the idea of "change for change's sake" and proves to those participating that closing an interaction gap was worth it. You could choose fixing an area where you need the most work or developing a new norm the team thinks will help it the most.

3) Work on developing new norms in the selected area until you nail it:

   • If you need to be educated in that area, get training or bring in a facilitator to help you out.

   • Identify behaviors that demonstrate that norm in action.

   • Identify creative ways to reinforce the new norms. (One team we know imposed a $5 fine on anyone who was late to meetings. Rather than being punitive, it became a group joke that was handled in a fun way but still conveyed the message that promptness would be a norm for the group.)

4) Once you see success and feel the norm is firmly established, pick another norm to work on.

---

6 Found at www2.3circlepartners.com/interaction-gap-resources

Balancing the Fun, Mundane, and Tricky

As you begin working through all of these techniques, the most critical factor will be making sure that any changes you adopt are an inside job. **Your group needs to have the power to shape its own norms.** So please use the advice and suggestions in this book as a guide and starting point, not a prescription that should be followed lockstep. Make it your own. Make the changes permanent by allowing and encouraging groups to opt in based on their desire and willingness to do so.

Remember, too, to step back and take a broad look at all three kinds of elements we've presented: the fun, mundane, and tricky. Engaging in the fun stuff creates enthusiasm and the incentive to keep going. More energy comes from tackling the mundane tasks—and especially from eliminating the barriers associated with doing the mundane stuff poorly. That energy is needed to help you overcome the natural reluctance to engage in interaction feedback and to deal with destructive conflict head on.

Eliminating any one of these ingredients can doom the effort to failure. If you only do the fun stuff, you'll have a hard time creating sustained change. Without tackling the mundane stuff, your energy can be sapped by unproductive meetings and a constant struggle with misalignment. If you avoid the tricky stuff, your groups will never get past the roadblocks to high performance.

What does all this mean in terms of pulling together a plan to make it happen? That's what we'll discuss in Part III.

Part III

Playing Three-Dimensional Chess

Pulling the Pieces Together

Throughout Part II, we reiterated the point that much of the work needed to close interaction gaps falls squarely into the "simple but not easy" category. The same descriptor applies to creating a plan for making improved interaction a reality: the steps to successful interaction are not particularly complicated to describe or even to implement, but pulling together a plan that works for you and those you work with, and then sustaining the recommended changes, can be challenging. People get excited and energized by the fun work and quick wins described in the previous section, but then falter once the fun turns into hard work that requires discipline to address the mundane stuff and the courage to deal with the tricky stuff.

We liken efforts to build interaction skills to embarking on a fitness program to counteract the effect of age, illness, or time on the couch. Both endeavors take persistence and discipline, and progress will often feel slow or nonexistent. Then, suddenly, one day you realize that you've accomplished your goal, and that encourages you to maintain the hard work so you don't slide backwards or to even set a new more ambitious goal.

There are a number of factors to consider as you plan for implementation. As with any major change, leadership engagement is crucial. Leaders can't simply initiate then delegate; they must participate and encourage. Second, as we discussed in Part II, you have to address changes at both the individual and team levels so you can change the group norms. Because of these factors, you have to approach interaction improvement as if it were a three-dimensional chess game and think about ways to integrate activities at three levels:

1) **You as the leader.** With few exceptions, much of a leader's ability to produce results is related to their impact on the people around them. A leader's behavior affects everything from the quality of decisions made to the ease of implementing changes and the ability of their employees to get work done quickly and efficiently. That's why a leader needs to start by working on their individual interaction skills. *See Chapter 9.*

2) **The group or team surrounding you.** We've noted several times that one way to sabotage or stifle interaction efforts is to work only on *individual* skills. Interaction improvement will happen more quickly and last much longer when you have the entire group or team working on the issues together. The best way to help improve your interaction skills is to involve the people around you—your home team—in the effort. *See Chapter 10.*

3) **The broader organization.** Resolving interaction problems within a group is an excellent start, but the biggest benefits from improved interaction come when the new ideas and methods are spread from a single group to entire departments and across the organization. Our primary piece of advice is NOT to create a separate "interaction initiative" but rather integrate it with other efforts and initiatives as an enabler or catalyst. This can happen in several ways. *See Chapter 11.*

—9—

Improving a Leader's "IQ" (Interaction Quotient)

Learning how you can best lead and interact with others

One of the main themes of this book is that all of us have an impact on how well the people around us interact with each other and with us. So all of us have a responsibility to pay attention to the things we do that increase or decrease interaction gaps—that is, the things that make it either harder or easier for others to contribute individually or as part of a team.

That message is particularly important for leaders. By definition, leaders have a degree of power and authority not available to other participants in an interaction. If you are in a leadership position, you should pose the question, "Are interaction gaps harming my effectiveness as a leader and/or the effectiveness of my team?" For most leaders the answer to that question is "Yes." They understand intuitively that improving their own skills in interaction will make them more effective. A leader who looks for opportunities to improve self-awareness gains a huge advantage in being able to execute all the other aspects of being an effective leader. How could it be otherwise? Knowledge is power, more knowledge is more power—and what better domain to have power in than understanding your strengths and weaknesses and the impact your behaviors have on others?

For most leaders, then, the challenge is to improve their **Interaction Quotient**: their knowledge of their own interaction strengths and weaknesses and their ability to promote more effective interaction in their groups or teams. Achieving both these goals is the subject of this chapter.

Tuning In to Your Interaction Style

There are three things extremely hard:
steel, a diamond, and to know one's self.

-Benjamin Franklin

A senior executive we once worked with believed that to be a good leader he had to set a good example and be willing to take on any task that he asked others to do. While on the surface this sounds like good "servant leadership," in reality this belief system and the actions that emerged from it caused this executive's teams to operate at half speed. He spent far too much time doing tasks he was not well suited for and not doing the things he really was good at.

Success for leaders lies in knowing themselves, acknowledging their own reality. That includes understanding what they do and don't bring to the table in terms of interaction, and using that knowledge to develop a leadership style all their own. We subscribe to the school of thought that there isn't any formula for an ideal leader: the secret to leadership effectiveness is being tuned in to your own unique style. That is fundamentally a more effective and satisfying approach than trying to change your personality to match someone else's definition of leadership.

The Team Role evaluation process described in Chapter 4 is a key step. That process provides information that is very hard for leaders to get by other means because people are usually so reluctant to provide feedback to bosses. Like others who go through this process, leaders will likely discover discrepancies between what they think of themselves and how others perceive them (the Ferraris in the garage or supposed Ferraris that should be parked). These discrepancies have a magnified impact on a group's effectiveness when the person lacking in self-knowledge is the leader. Here's one example:

Ruth was an HR director who saw herself as very analytical, impartial, and capable of applying highly rational logic. She did not think of herself as particularly extroverted or energetic.

The perceptions of people who worked directly for her or served on teams she led were the exact opposite. They didn't think much of her analytical skills, but found her to be a dynamic, very outgoing person who was an excellent cheerleader (good at encouraging others and keeping energy levels high). Perhaps she was a bit over-optimistic at times, but the energy she brought to her teams was invaluable.

This mismatch between Ruth's self-perceptions and other's perceptions of her was the source of friction. She couldn't understand why her staff was continually looking to others to help with analysis, and was frustrated when they would go behind her back even if she offered to help with that work.

Once her co-workers shared their perceptions with Ruth, she was able to change her behavior based on a better understanding of her strengths and weaknesses. Though initially disappointed that others did not value her analytical skills, she realized that her ability to read people's situations quickly and accurately and be seen as a supporter of others' development was an asset in her job. In fact, she realized she loved doing that kind of work on a team. This new understanding of her abilities had a lasting effect on her approach to dealing with others and dramatically improved the results her teams

achieved. Her improved personal effectiveness also contrib-
uted to an upswing in her career.

The degree of match between an individual's self-perception and the perception of others is what we term **coherence**. Ruth initially had a low degree of coherence: her perception of her strengths was very different from what other people thought. Think about the impact of this situation. Ruth had spent her career downplaying strengths that she could have brought to the teams she worked with. As a consequence, she had also been robbing her groups of a contribution she could have made, and had to deal with the frustration she felt when her teams did not embrace her interest in doing the analytical work.

A leader with low coherence will have a hard time achieving fully productive relationships with the people in their sphere of influence. They are likely to be more defensive, which is antithetical to creating a learning environment. In contrast, we have found that generally the higher degree of coherence, the greater the effectiveness of a leader, for reasons we'll discuss shortly.

Evaluating coherence

You can evaluate coherence in a variety of ways, both formal and informal. Not surprisingly, we favor a formal analytical method based on the data generated through the Team Role analysis. We start by comparing how often a person's top three Team Roles match the top roles perceived by the other people who are evaluating them. A perfect match between a person's self-rated top-three roles and the top-three roles as evaluated by others would give a coherence score of 100%. A perfect mismatch (no overlap between self-perception and others' perception) would generate a coherence score of 0%.

A random sampling of coherence scores from our database is shown in Figure 18. As you can see, the median was below 50%.

That means less than half the time what an individual thought of as a strength was not perceived that way by others, and vice versa (the other evaluators perceived strengths the individual did not rate as highly).

Figure 18: Evaluating Coherence

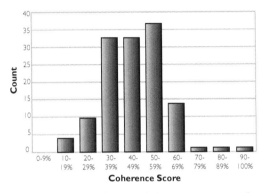

The higher the score, the better the match between a person's self-ratings and the ratings from others.

In general, someone who improves their coherence improves their leadership effectiveness. Coherent leaders have a very accurate view of their strengths and weaknesses, meaning their self-perception is very much in line with how others see them. They are personally more effective because they spend more time playing to their strengths and less time on work they are not very good at.

Furthermore, bosses, peers, co-workers, and employees generally have more trust in a coherent leader because that person behaves in consistent, expected ways. When leaders are surrounded by people who know about their strengths and their weaknesses, they are less likely to be defensive and less likely to create defensiveness in others. Experiencing the empowerment from their greater self-awareness gives a coherent leader more incentive to invest in the growth of their direct reports.

Highly coherent, but anti-interaction

While higher coherence opens the door for improved interaction, it doesn't guarantee it. For example, we worked with Scott, a manager with a coherence score of over 90%. That meant the way he perceived his strengths was very close to how others viewed him. However, what Scott knew, and what everyone around him also knew, was that he had a big ego and believed in his own brilliance. He could be counted on to push his own agenda and take credit for the contributions of direct reports. Because everyone knew these things about Scott, there were no surprises when he behaved in accordance with his views. People tried to interact with him as little as possible. In short, Scott's high coherence was around behaviors that made effective interaction impossible.

Capitalize on your strengths; Embrace your weaknesses

The self-knowledge we champion in this book gives leaders greater awareness of their strengths and weaknesses. The most obvious consequence of this knowledge is the expectation that they will take on work that leverages their strengths. But just what are their true strengths? As we've discussed many times in this book, most of us have a false perception of what we do well and what we are poor at in terms of interaction. So when we advise people to "play to your strengths," we specifically mean the interaction strengths *that others perceive in them* (that is, strengths confirmed by the observations of others), not what the person thinks they are good at. The more time people devote to building on their true strengths, the better they get in those areas and the less time they'll spend on tasks that they're not good at. It's a win-win all around.

Much more challenging than playing to strengths, however, is dealing with weaknesses. It is fair to say that everyone brings certain weaknesses to the way in which they interact with others. Perhaps it's impulsiveness, rigidity, a lack of follow through, or being inattentive to priorities. Capitalizing on our strengths is, for most of us, a fairly straightforward proposition; managing our allowable weaknesses and ensuring they do not become dis-allowable can be far more challenging and important in the long run, especially for leaders.

As we discussed in Chapter 4, some weaknesses are allowable because they are part of the package that includes a corresponding strength. You won't get far if you try to fight against your allowable weaknesses, and you will never be able to correct them to the point where they go away entirely. That doesn't give you a green light to ignore your weaknesses. Indulging a weakness can make it "dis-allowable" by interfering with interaction in your sphere of influence.

If you are a leader, embrace the fact that your weaknesses will be challenging for you. You must be open about that fact and engage those around you in helping you manage any weaknesses. Be clear about ground rules so that others can point out to you when a weakness starts to interfere with your ability to conduct work.

A personal example from one of the authors helps to illustrate this idea:

> *Throughout my professional career I have been poor at paying attention to details and providing consistent follow up. It didn't quite hit the level of a fatal flaw, but that deficit was always noted in my performance reviews. So, for years, when my boss told me I needed to pay more attention to detail, I would go out and spend a frustrating period where I consciously reminded myself to think about details. Of course, not only did I **not** get any better, I was so preoccupied that I was not focusing on my strengths either.*
>
> *After learning about the Team Roles, I came to understand that my strengths and weakness were part of the same package. It was a big relief to learn that I could only get so far in my attempts to fix these things that had been pointed out as weaknesses. So, I turned my attention to trying to manage them and make sure neither I nor my teams suffered because of them.*

> Now, I make sure that my teams know that I'm not great at detail work, and I always want to have one or two people around me who **are** very strong in that area. Whenever possible, I find an assistant who is highly meticulous and lets nothing slip through the cracks.
>
> There are times, however, when I have no choice but to dive into the details on a project or task. I no longer try to kid myself that it will be a piece of cake. I know it will be extremely hard for me. So I carve out a chunk of time—usually three times longer than I think it should take—and then when I'm finished I give myself some sort of reward (time on an activity I enjoy, a nice glass of wine, etc.).
>
> Just embracing the fact that I really am poor at the details and actually being very comfortable letting people I work with know about this weakness of mine has turned out to be an effective management strategy. It avoids much frustration and ensures that my lack of detail-orientation doesn't hinder my effectiveness or that of my teams.

This is what embracing weaknesses looks like. You openly acknowledge the areas where you are not great, and make sure that you have a support system to cover those areas as much as possible.

Continuous Learning

One of the best ways to improve your effectiveness as a leader is to continually learn how to better interact with others around you, be they those you report to, peers, or people who report to you. We talked about the basics of learning in Part II and below we have gathered some special tips in this area for leaders.

Invite feedback

We made the point earlier that none of us can truly know what impact we have on others unless those people are willing to tell us. Feedback from others helps us crystallize in our mind when and how we can best use our own skills and what areas we should work on in ourselves. Each of us must therefore be open to hearing feedback, and create an environment where others are willing to give it.

Leaders have to go the extra mile to solicit input because most people are understandably wary to speak openly to someone they view as a boss. One essential skill for leaders, therefore, is the technique of disclosure discussed in Chapter 7. An employee or even a peer will feel much more comfortable speaking up if a leader starts a conversation by asking for their opinion about a specific subject the leader wants feedback on.

Disclosure also helps leaders because it allows them to take control over a situation where they might otherwise feel vulnerable or to get help with an issue without having to confess their ignorance. We can't count the number of times that managers have told us, "As a leader, you can't say you don't know what you're doing. You'll look stupid. As the leader, you're supposed to know." With disclosure, you can admit uncertainty in a way that engages others in helping you find a solution: "I've been concerned about XYZ, and wanted to get your thoughts." By disclosing a concern, you lower the risk for the feedback giver—they now know that you're interested in hearing their thoughts.

One final tip: If you repeatedly receive feedback about a specific concern that people have about your behavior, then it's unlikely you will be able to change the situation on your own. You will have to engage the people around you—your staff, a peer, or colleague—in helping you recognize when you are falling into old behavior patterns, and then have a plan of attack for how to change when that happens. Someone has to have the power to say, "You're doing it again," without fearing that you will react negatively. Old habits die hard, as the saying goes. It really helps when others around you are comfortable pointing out when we slip into old patterns of behavior.

Be vigilant about your non-verbal signals

Leaders have to be extremely watchful of any non-verbal messages they send, especially when receiving feedback. A manager once told us that he had recently moved to a new company that had a much more open and honest culture than his previous organization. After he had been there about three months, one of his direct reports said to him, "I'm not sure why, but I find it difficult to give you feedback. It's not anything particular that you say or do, I just get this vibe that you're not really interested in it."

The manager said he had a good discussion with that employee and explored the notion that he was unwelcoming to feedback with other team members. He told us, "I discovered that I was seen as friendly but guarded. So I had to really watch what I said and, more importantly, my facial expressions and body language whenever someone was giving me feedback, to demonstrate that I was truly interested in what they had to say."

Be on the alert for defensiveness

The reluctance that most people have to be frank when they deal with authority figures is also the reason why leaders have to be so careful about not reacting defensively when receiving feedback or criticism. If they give even the slightest hint through gestures, expressions, or words that they don't want to hear the feedback, they will successfully cut off all input from their team or colleagues—and lose out on information vital to self-mastery.

More importantly, a leader prone to defensive reactions creates an environment where the chances for improved interaction are almost nil. Their defensive reactions cause those around them to be defensive as well. As we talked about earlier in the book, when everyone in a group is being defensive, people keep ideas to themselves and aren't open to learning. This mini-silo effect expands interaction gaps and hinders effectiveness.

As a leader, then, you must be vigilant in guarding against defensiveness, especially in situations where that reaction is almost expected (when we are unsure about a situation or when someone provides unsolicited input in the middle of a meeting, for example).

Increase Your Versatility

The best leaders we know are very versatile, adapting their management and interaction style based on the situation. Often (but not always), the worst leaders are people who are stuck in a style rut. They have a "One Size Fits All" preferred way of interacting and of solving problems.

We talked about how knowledge of preferred and manageable Team Roles can make anyone more versatile. That knowledge, coupled with interaction feedback, is particularly helpful for anyone who is a leader—it helps them do what many natural leaders do intuitively, namely, adapt their management style by using different approaches in different circumstances, which is the hallmark of versatility.

For example, at one point a manager we know was in a meeting that seemed to be going nowhere because several key people (including her) were trying to steer the meeting. Though coordination of efforts was one of her Team Role strengths, she realized that focusing on that role in that particular meeting was a mistake. So, she consciously stopped focusing on that set of skills and instead focused on steps that would help the group as a whole make progress.

As another example, we worked with an executive who prided himself on keeping everyone informed of corporate decisions or issues. He was known as one to call a meeting at the drop of a hat. Through feedback, he learned that most of his staff saw this tendency as a waste of time and effort, so he became much more judicious about holding meetings—with an instant payback in terms of his own and his staff's productivity.

Like any other skill, versatility comes naturally to some people but most of us have to consciously work at it. Obviously, we recommend that you evaluate your Team Roles; once you fully internalize the various team roles at which you excel, you will be better able to deliberately decide to play (or not play) certain roles.

Promoting Better Interaction Around You

So far in this chapter, we've talked about what you can do to become more effective in how you interact with others. A leader, however, also has to take into account the influence they can have on the group as a whole, and pay attention to how they are promoting or hindering interaction in their teams. What a leader does or doesn't say, the way they behave, their body language and tone of voice, the decisions they make about who gets assigned what responsibilities . . . all of this affects every aspect of how the people around them accomplish their work, including:

- How decisions are shaped (what kind of information is available, how people see their roles in making a decision, etc.)

- How people treat each other

- Motivation and commitment

- Trust levels and respect

- People's comfort in expressing their opinions

- People's ability to contribute to their group

- How conflict is handled

In your role as a leader, you have the power to create an environment where all of these aspects of interaction are handled effectively. The starting point is making sure there is respect on all sides and establishing ground rules that encompass common civility. Beyond that, there are four specific ways to apply concepts introduced earlier in this book to create a workplace where effective interaction becomes a norm.

Increase your mastery of the fundamentals

Many managers and executives have been through leadership development processes that include instruction on basic interaction concepts, but it's easy for those skills to get rusty if they aren't used regularly. One of the first steps in developing an environment of effective interaction is to do a self-check against the lessons you may have learned before about interaction (many of which were embedded in the Fun, Mundane, and Tricky topics in Part II). For example:

- Do you practice active listening skills?

- Do you use inquiry skills to get people to say more about what they are thinking?

- In meetings, do you make sure that everyone gets a chance to state their ideas and that no one is suppressed?

- Do you invite and welcome feedback? Do you go to great lengths to make sure you aren't reacting defensively?

- Do you help to foster productive conflict? (Or do you shun conflict or allow destructive conflict?)

- Do you make sure that there is purpose to each meeting or discussion?

Keep interaction front & center

You can't improve interaction if you ignore it . . . and if you ignore it, so will your team. One of the roles of a leader, therefore, is to keep the goal of improving interaction front and center. Doing this needn't be complicated. You can, for example, use the tactic introduced in Chapter 5 for doing brief checks on interaction at the end of meetings. These checks can be either open-ended ("What did we do well today?") or focused on specific interaction issues identified by your team ("Have we been clear enough about the purpose for each meeting?").

Second, raise the subject of interaction effectiveness in the everyday discussions you have with co-workers or staff. Ask your teams to demonstrate that all members have a shared understanding of the team's purpose. Challenge them to think about whether poor interaction could be contributing to problems they see in daily work.

Third, treat interaction just as you would any other key aspect of business: identify challenges and have a plan of attack (more on this in the next chapter). Then do periodic reviews on progress, identify roadblocks, and take corrective action.

Know thy team

Jonathon is the head of a sales organization. He has several regional sales managers who report directly to him (they have dotted-line reporting relationships to the presidents of the var-

ious regions in the company). He also has a team of people at the head office that provide support to the regions. Jonathon analyzed the various relationships between all these players and reached several important conclusions.

For example, prior to this analysis, he had thought of his regional sales managers as a team. Afterwards, he realized that they were not truly a team in the traditional sense. In fact, the sales managers were somewhat in competition with each other and had almost no interdependencies. Jonathon realized he needed to view himself as a "leader of leaders" when dealing with the sales managers, and that his best approach would be for him to develop much closer one-on-one relationships with each of them. Consequently, he also revamped the structure of the monthly meetings so more appropriate communication and sharing of information could occur.

For the head office team, Jonathon adopted a different approach because they were a more cohesive group. He took the necessary steps to develop the team's interaction skills and turn them into a high-performance team.

Jonathon's experience represents one way in which leaders can shape better effectiveness: by understanding the connections and relationships between the people and groups in their sphere of influence.

A second strategy is to use knowledge of the collaborative strengths and weaknesses on the team to help them decide who should be involved (and how) in what tasks and decisions. That helps leaders better use the resources around them and is a win-win situation when done effectively. For example, you could approach a creative person on your staff and say, "I'm stuck on this project and I would love to hear some of those great ideas you come up with." First off, that person is likely to be delighted that you are asking for their help and will be highly likely to provide a quality response. Second, by acknowledging that you see the person as creative, you help to improve that person's own self-awareness—providing feedback without ever using the word "feedback"!

Better knowledge of the collective strengths and weaknesses on your team will also help you decide what level of interaction is needed to achieve your unit's goals. You may not need any (you make a decision on your own), but often you will need at least a little if not a lot of interaction with a few people or the whole unit.

Find ways to lower defensiveness

One of the best ways to improve the overall effectiveness of interaction in your team or organization is to create an environment where people's level of defensiveness is very low. To do that, work to adopt principles that foster an open exchange of information and ideas. That includes ideas we've discussed several times:

- Working from valid information regardless of who contributes it.

- Playing to people's strengths and managing weaknesses.

- Openly discussing interaction issues with the team and making sure that all voices are heard.

- Focusing on learning how to improve interaction, not blaming people for perceived problems.

This will lead to an environment where there is real openness and people actually listen to understand—avoiding the "hearing but not listening" trap that is so easy to fall into.

Improved Leadership Effectiveness

Time and again, leaders have told us how much more effective they are when they work on improving their Interaction Quotient. Having a clear understanding of their own interaction strengths and weaknesses, allows them to put their abilities to optimal use, and to do the same with the people who report to them. That improves the quality of not only the everyday mundane exchanges between colleagues—discussions, sharing of information, analysis—but cumulatively leads to a better understanding of what's going on in the workplace and business, which leads to better decisions and smoother implementation. That's the positive spiral created by having a higher IQ.

—10—

Start with the Home Team

The most common model for providing skill training in business is to take individuals out of their work environment, cram great ideas and techniques into their heads, and then send them back to the job expecting them to apply those new skills automatically.

If you've read the chapters in Part II, you know why improving interaction doesn't work that way. The only way to improve interaction is to focus on what happens when the people you need to work with every day are actually *interacting* with each other. It is the team's behavior, not just the individual's, that has to change to bring about different results from better interaction—because it's the group's norms that have to shift, not just individual habits. If you don't change the behavior of the group, the old patterns of interaction will never lose their grip.

Further, the impact of any work on interaction will be limited unless you create a shared group experience for the people involved in the interactions you want to improve. New norms are easier to develop when everyone in a group is reinforcing the application of new methods of interacting.

The most logical starting point for driving a new norm around interaction is to begin working with the group you think of as your "home team." That could be your everyday work team, a key project team you serve on, or perhaps a problem-solving team of some sort. There are three steps to the process:

1. Establish a current state of interaction and identify pain points.

2. Develop individual interaction skills.

3. Have the team define its own future and develop an interaction plan for how to get there.

We'll go through these steps in this chapter, then provide two case studies to illustrate how they work in the real world.

Step 1. Current State and Pain Points

When we ask people to tell us how many high-performing teams they've been on, many people reply, "None." The fortunate ones say, "One or two." The frequency of underperforming teams is so prevalent that it's no wonder most people are skeptical that anything different is possible.

This is a huge barrier to overcome, and it explains why theory or logic alone doesn't create the motivation to improve interaction. You can talk until you're blue in the face about the value of cooperation or the logic of improving interaction or why there is a "burning platform for change," and, for the most part, very little happens. We've seen leaders try to rally the troops through cheerleading many times and the results rarely fail to disappoint. You have probably seen it, too. The motivation to improve interaction cannot be forced on anyone; it is theirs to give, not yours to take, as the saying goes. People have to come to a realization themselves that they want to change, and if you try to force the issue, you'll only get compliance not commitment. (If your doctor diagnosed a problem but you were firmly convinced that there was nothing you could do to fix it, you probably wouldn't even try, would you?)

"Burning platforms" don't provide the motivation to improve interaction

One of the business trends in the past decade is using a "burning platform" to motivate the workforce. We agree that having a good business reason for taking action is also a necessary ingredient for investing in an effort to improve interaction. However, as you saw with the product development team in Chapter 1, which was very late in completing a critical new product, simply having a business imperative for results isn't enough by itself to force effective collaboration.

Being able to shape your business needs into a burning platform statement is great for describing where your *organization* needs to be (and, perhaps, the dire consequences if the goal isn't met), but it rarely relates to people at a *personal* level. There is seldom a direct "What's in it for me?" aspect to burning platforms; and it's that personal WIIFM that makes people willing to at least explore changing their own behavior to improve interaction.

In addition, in our experience, leaders can sometimes use the urgency embodied in a burning platform as an excuse to force changes on people—and you cannot force people to improve interaction. They have to *want* to change.

From our observation, the pattern is clear: **no one will be motivated to fix a problem they don't see.** Nothing positive can happen *until and unless* people recognize that their current method of interacting is hindering their effectiveness. Having a problem you can clearly link to a lack of effective interaction has to be the starting point of the journey.

That's why to begin work on improving interaction within a group, you have to give people an experience that gives them a gut-level feeling that *something better is possible*. The experience should also provide the opportunity for them to identify the specific interaction areas the group wants to improve. People have to believe that if they put in effort, something they care about will change for the better.

There are many ways to provide an experience that will motivate people to improve interaction. We usually design processes built around the simulation described in Chapter 1. As a quick recap, we divide participants into ad hoc teams of about five people and put them through a series of business scenarios where they have to make decisions. Between each scenario, they receive training on the building blocks of effective interaction, which we've covered in previous chapters, including:

- Understanding the Team Roles (where people get to find the Ferraris in their garage and learn how to manage their weaknesses)

- Effective advocacy & inquiry

- The importance of using ground rules

- Feedback at both the individual and group levels

Through this blend of instruction and decision-making rounds, people both see and experience firsthand the following changes:

- They realize they simply accepted poor collaboration at first, not recognizing it as a problem.

- They see that in every round the *individual* scores are lower than the *team* scores. That is, there were resources on the team that could have helped the group achieve a better result, but they failed to recognize and utilize them.

- Even the hardest skeptics have to admit that a team performs at its best when all members contribute, not just those with the most seniority or the loudest voices.

- While most people are uncomfortable at first dealing directly with interaction (such as providing and listening to feedback), they became more and more comfortable even over just the few days of the workshop. They realized that being open to dealing with interaction directly is not as big a deal as they thought.

As part of the workshop, we also establish a baseline of interaction effectiveness by having everyone score their team on multiple dimensions of interaction (such as goal setting, planning, use of data, and so on).

Through this work, the team discovers what resources it has to work with and begins to expose its interaction pain points. We've given a number of examples of typical pain points in the examples throughout this book, including the oft-cited product development teams from Chapter 1. Here are a few other pain points we've heard from actual teams:

- "We have too many people involved in this work, and not enough structure, clarity, or alignment."

- "Our core team is too large and no one's clear about its purpose."

- "Our project teams start out with a clear focus, but we see 'scope creep' and the timelines keep getting longer and longer."

- "This team is famous in the organization for delivering results late and over budget."

What's important about these pain points is that they were specific to the groups involved, so everyone around them could associate the interaction pain point with something they experienced on the job. Interestingly, many of the people directly involved did not at first recognize the interaction component of these problems; others did not think that improvement was possible. But because they acknowledged a problem that affected them personally, the majority of people were willing to take deliberate steps to improve interaction.

Step 2. Individual Interaction Skills

Though interaction by definition involves more than one person, improving interaction relies on having a strong foundation of *individual* interaction skills. The discovery work in Step 1 (establishing a current state and identifying pain points) will likely reveal challenges the group faces in terms of effective collaboration, but each individual will likely find areas where they can improve.

We recommend that people develop individual action plans that spell out specifically how they want to get better—such as building up an area of strength, managing a weakness, or inviting feedback. Ideally, they will share their goals with the teams and work groups so that others around them can help support their development.

Step 3. A Team Interaction Plan

The first two steps in this process have created a baseline of knowledge and skills that provides a solid platform from which to build. Once the people you work with understand more about interaction, you can collectively work to define what interaction on your team should look like in the future and develop a plan for getting there.

To help teams think through the issues they need to address, we studied the characteristics and behaviors of high-performing teams. They have many elements in place that keep them moving forward, prevent them from wasting time and talent, and help them quickly overcome barriers. Making sure those elements are in place not only creates a high degree of alignment but also helps the team build trust because they know that everyone will be operating from the same foundation. Below is a list of basic issues your team should address. You may think of additional topics needed to foster better interaction in your specific environment.

A. Team Purpose. You'd be surprised how common it is for team members to think they have a shared understanding of their team's purpose only to discover that everyone has a different interpretation. So, as obvious as it may sound, a team should always start out by discussing fundamental questions such as, "Why do we exist?" and "What does success look like for us as a team?" The goal is to identify a purpose that is directly relevant to the people on the team (not just an abstraction) and that everyone agrees on.

B. Guiding Principles. Guiding principles help keep the team on track throughout their time together. These principles link the team's purpose to its tactics. Guiding principles often describe the team's aspirations and values and/or clearly define what the team will or won't do in the way they operate together. Some examples from real teams include:

- We will support, challenge and hold each other accountable

- Seek first to understand and assume best intent

- Leverage each other's strengths

C. Collaboration and Meetings. Often, teams take *how* they work together for granted, an attitude that can contribute to big interaction gaps. We advise teams to talk about collaboration and make sure what they are doing is helping them achieve their team's purpose and goals. They should, for example, talk about the frequency, length, and content of their meetings, and decide if changes in any of these factors could make the team operate more effectively.

D. Team Alignment on Roles and Responsibilities. In order to galvanize a team and ensure that it capitalizes on individual strengths, there needs to be a discussion about the contribution that each person brings to the team. Part of that discussion should be based on the Team Role framework we've referenced many times. The output will be a document that captures each member's strengths to build on, areas of weakness to manage, and how team members will help each other. Another part of the discussion should be centered on who will be responsible for what tasks at the core of the team's purpose—whether that is running a process, creating plans, designing a product or service, or solving problems.

E. Ground Rules. Every group takes on a unique character and pattern of interaction based on the norms it adopts (consciously or unconsciously). Developing explicit ground rules increases the likelihood of the team operating as intended because it provides a frame of reference to evaluate how meetings and interactions are going. That way, problems can be recognized and resolved more quickly.

F. Implementation & Learning Practices. The decisions made around the first five topics won't do much good if the team doesn't also discuss how it will implement these decisions and continue learning and improving in each area. So, the team also needs to answer the following questions:

- How can we make sure we act in ways consistent with our principles?

- What can we do with the Team Map to make sure we continue to emphasize strengths and manage weaknesses?

- How will we reinforce our norms?

The process of working through these issues is critical because the group is working collectively to define its own future. That way, all members will have an equal stake in supporting the decisions the group reaches. By discussing these issues, the team is creating a shared understanding of the group's rules of the road and developing an interaction plan that defines a better future.

Remember—Think Fitness, Not Dieting

One of the hallmarks of a high functioning team is its ability to keep learning and adapting. The process we use integrates individual improvement plans and team level interaction planning that makes sure the mundane and tricky stuff are not forgotten.

As we alluded to earlier, the metaphor we use with groups once they've passed the initial phases of discovery is "think fitness, not dieting." Improving interaction is akin to improving fitness; it's a lifestyle choice. Unlike traditional diets that you can go on and off, fitness (and interaction) requires commitment, discipline, and persistence. The result is very predictable and straightforward in one sense: if you invest the time and effort you will see results, if you don't, you won't—it really is that simple!

Making It Real:
Case Studies in Team Development

The three steps outlined above will play out in different ways depending on the situation and need. Here are two examples that show how the pieces can come together.

Case 1: Operations team

When a new COO took over the struggling operations team in one division of a consumer products company, he wanted to turn them into a high-performance team. To begin, he had his team work through the foundational elements described above, and together the team agreed to a number of immediate changes.

For example, historically, the members of the team saw their role as representing their individual departments. Now, they all agreed that the main purpose of the team was to make sure the resources of this division were used most effectively. To do that, the individual managers would have to sometimes set aside their notion of what would be best for their departments and instead look at what would be best for the division as a whole.

The team also decided to change the frequency and duration of their meetings. Originally, they had been meeting for two hours once a month but when the team reviewed the full range of its responsibilities, they realized they needed to meet for a half-day every two to three weeks. They also decided that two VPs would rotate the responsibility for developing draft agendas for the meetings because they were better suited to that task than the COO.

In analyzing the Team Map, the team discovered that overall there was a good balance of all three types of roles (Thinking, Action, People). However, there was an overabundance in two Thinking roles (which led to over-analyzing) and one Action role (where the strong personalities tended to clash). This helped explain one of the reasons the team had struggled in the past: they'd had seemingly endless discussions but no one ever changed their minds! They would almost always end up agreeing to disagree (meaning no decisions were actually made).

To deal with these issues, the team realized that they would need to have a ground rule that all team members should feel free to talk openly about points of frustration, and that they would need a solid mechanism for conflict resolution. You can see this team's ground rules in Figure 19.

After these changes were made, the operations team reported a marked improvement in what was accomplished, which led to much greater satisfaction with their meetings. They were far clearer on what needed to happen in each meeting, were better at balancing their focus on strategic and tactical issues, and had mechanisms that helped them get past their former interaction roadblocks. As a result, they made faster progress, and saw improved effectiveness across their division. They also started to actually enjoy their meetings (how many people can say that?).

Figure 19: Operations Team Ground Rules for Meetings

Goal setting & alignment	• First 15 mins. of every meeting to clarify and confirm the goals (purpose) of that meeting
Processes	• Create draft of next agenda at the end of each meeting • Agenda published 1 week in advance • Explicitly show expected action
Responsibility	• Assign meeting leader, facilitator, scribe, timekeeper • Include check on previous meeting Action Items
Data	• PowerPoints to be no more than 5 slides; to include exec summary • Bring data to justify recommendations
Handling conflict & making decisions	• Always define the objective up front and the input requested • Topic Facilitator to request that conflict be taken offline or resolved at that moment • Process for resolving conflict must be "round the table"
Learning & feedback	• Set aside time in the agenda for quick check at the end • Commit to do a Learning Cycle as needed

Case 2: Technology development team

A technology company that was already established in the U.S. and Mexico wanted to make a strategic move by creating a new product for the European market. The goal was particularly ambitious for a company that had not released an update for their product in more than 10 years!

The timeline was tight and the three teams required for this task would have to do better at achieving key milestones than they had ever done in the past. One of the three teams, which we'll call Team Galaxy, had a poor reputation within the company. Half the team members were part of a disbanded team that on three separate projects had failed to produce the required deliverables on time and on budget.

To make the situation worse, the team culture within this company was lacking in rigor as well as personal and professional accountability: even if people recognized impending problems, the standard way of dealing with them was to stand by and wait to see what happened, then try to find someone else to blame. Few teams paid more than lip service to their charters.

Despite Team Galaxy's particular history and the poor team culture in the organization, the members were able to completely overhaul their approach by working on a number of interaction issues, which allowed them to work faster and better. They created a new foundation of inter-action built on the elements we described above and listed below:

1. **Guiding principles**. They reached a number of agreements describing how the team would do its work (see sidebar for examples). As a result, the team members now operate from a shared viewpoint of accountability, not just individually but collectively.

Team Galaxy Guiding Principles

- We learn from our successes and failures. We identify successes/ failures as soon as they are visible, and identify what we can learn from them. We document our successes and our failures.

- We offer feedback to team members, and we act on feedback we receive from others. Feedback is defined as an open dialogue about anything project related directed to the betterment of the team. Feedback includes topics such as technical decisions, business decisions, and interaction. Feedback is not taken personally. We do not retaliate.

- We take accountability, ownership, and do not blame others.

- We reach out to our team members to help each other and our team succeed.

- We ask others for help if we are struggling with something.

---

2. **Agreeing on a purpose.** Over the course of several meetings, Team Galaxy members discussed different options for the vision of the product components they were charged with developing. The resulting vision statement provided a reference point the team used to gauge progress and to validate if they were still on the same path or if they needed to adjust their work.

3. **Analyzing its Team Role composition at both an individual and team level.** The analysis of Team Galaxy's Team Map led to three insights:

   a) **The team had an overabundance of Thinking skills.** Normally, this poses the risk that a team is too easily distracted by ideas, but here the "extra thinking power" was useful because the team was able to focus its creativity on *solutions*.

   b) **The team was weak in the People skills.** After reviewing past team experiences, Team Galaxy members realized that many problems had stemmed from the lack of attention to what was happening on the team at a personal level. This time around, they would benefit if the people who did *not* have good People skills did more to support those who did.

   c) **The project manager (PM) was the most action-oriented of the team members but weak in the People skills.** She was often seen as abrasive and demanding by others because she was so focused on getting work done and making deadlines. However, the team realized that without this action focus, they would never get anything done. They came to accept and even appreciate the PM's action-bias and her need to make tough calls when they fell behind or struggled to make deadlines (even though it often felt uncomfortable in the moment).

4. **Clarifying team responsibilities.** In this company, teams did not usually discuss each member's responsibilities. However, Team Galaxy realized that lack of information had created problems in the past. To deal with this, each team member completed a list of their responsibilities on the team (the tasks or jobs they performed). The lists were emailed to the whole team, then reviewed and discussed at a team meeting until all the roles and responsibilities were agreed on. As a result, nowadays tasks seldom fall through the gaps (which used to happen all the time), and there is very little duplication of effort (another common problem). The team was also able to identify "single points of failure"—critical skills that would be lost if a person left the team for any reason. Cross-training and identification of back-ups eliminated the possibility that the loss of anyone with critical skills would cripple the team.

5. **Risk planning.** While this element is not part of our standard list of topics for teams, many find themselves in situations where risk management is key to success. That was the case for Team Galaxy, so they reviewed a list of problems that had occurred in previous projects, which included problems such as team inflexibility, a lack of clear definition of the desired product features, challenges working with 3rd party vendors, a disengaged team member, and unclear communication between team members. Every problem was put up on a "Pitfall Plaza" (left side of Figure 20) and the team discussed each and brainstormed counter-actions. If the threat was neutralized, the items were moved to the "Safe Zone" (right side of Figure 20).

6. **Continuous improvement.** The team started doing regular checks of how well they were performing on a range of team effectiveness dimensions.

Figure 20: Pitfall Plaza and Safe Zone

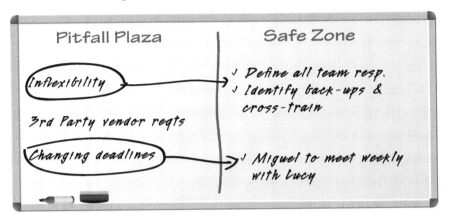

Going through all six of these topics may sound like a lot of work, but in total, it only took the team about 10 hours, which they interspersed with "real work" over a period of six months. The further they got, the more benefits they saw. For example, one team member volunteered to perform a set of critical tasks. It wasn't until just before the deadline that the team realized the person didn't have the skills to do the job correctly. Instead of blaming the volunteer, the team members agreed that the problem was, in large part, the team's fault for not being more careful in assigning the tasks, and everyone pitched in (and worked some very long hours) to solve the problem.

Enforcing the new standards did not come easily. At first, team members looked at their continuous improvement reviews as busywork. But they soon learned that the measurements gave them a starting point for having productive discussions of how to operate better both individually and as a team. As a result of all this work, the team now completes its work much faster, and the quality has improved by 80% based on a set of internal metrics. In fact, the team is now famous for delivering on time and under budget.

An Individual and Collective Experience

Interaction is always a collective experience between people, whether it's a one-on-one discussion, team meeting, or formal collaboration between groups or departments. For that reason, learning to improve interaction will only be successful if it is approached as a collective effort. However, the effort usually needs to be driven by, or at the very least strongly supported by, the operational or team leader. If you are in a leadership position, begin to work on these issues with your home team. Not everyone will be convinced or excited at first, but usually they become engaged quickly after they see and experience the benefits of better interaction.

The rewards of putting in the effort to build a high-performance team are definitely worth the sustained effort. When we ask people to tell us about what their teams are like now, they tend to get pretty passionate:

- "We got the product out a week early and 15% under budget!"

- "We worked all hours to make it happen, but everyone was pulling their weight."

- "We really challenged each other and sometimes we weren't even sure we would make the deadline. But each time a different team member would step up and keep us going. It was amazing!"

The consistent theme we see in teams or groups that achieve this level of performance is that they make closing interaction gaps an ongoing priority and fully commit to planning and reviewing progress.

— 11 —

Three Deployment Options

One of the clearest lessons from our past two decades in this field is that interaction is an area that doesn't easily lend itself to raise-the-roof rallying cries. For that reason, the best way to make progress on interaction is to not treat it as a big change initiative unto itself.

Effective interaction is like the oil that makes it easier for gears to do their work; in this case, those gears are strategy and execution. So look for gears in your organization that are clogged or sticky, and use a focus on interaction to help them mesh more easily. In general, this leads to four approaches:

1) Using interaction practices to conquer cross-functional barriers (**silo busting**)

2) Adding an interaction component to another existing initiative or major project (a **booster shot** for enabling greater success of that initiative)

3) & 4) Using an evolutionary model, allowing interaction growth to occur organically by either **cascading it down** (start at the top and have the leaders take it to their teams, who then take it down to the next level, etc.) or letting it **go viral** at its own pace (building off the success of any individual team by allowing their success to create interest in other groups).

We'll give examples of all these approaches in this chapter.

Silo Busting

One of the most common reasons why companies focus on interaction processes is to overcome problems that are hindering major cross-functional efforts. If you've had turf wars or silo clashes in your organization, you know how painful these can be.

For one last time, we'll reference the product design group from Chapter 1, which was essentially a cross-functional team combining the cowboy and geek silos. The two groups had managed to get work done when the stakes were low but fell apart when the stakes and pressure were much greater. The same thing happened to a U.S. consumer goods company that has been in the enviable position of seeing rapid growth in recent years and which therefore needed to add production lines to keep up with increased demand and the fast pace of new product launches.

As you might expect, many different functional groups are involved in these kinds of projects, including the design and engineering group, the installation and operations (manufacturing) group, and even the sales and marketing departments (because the increased output is an enabler of better revenues). As with the cowboy/geek company, these groups had managed to get work done when the pace was slow, but discovered that the underlying problems caused enormous headaches when they had to ratchet up the pace and scope of efforts.

A few years ago, the VPs in charge of the latest production line expansion approached us and said, "We were able to get the last line built on time and on budget, but it was an incredibly painful experience. Now we have to build two more state-of-the-art production lines and we definitely do NOT want to go through that same painful experience again! Can you help?"

The VPs went on to explain that they thought they had solid processes in place because they'd successfully added production lines in the past. Now, in their words, "people problems" were making the work extremely difficult. We asked them what they meant by people problems and they came up with a lot of examples. What follows are some highlights:

The VPs admitted that in hindsight several key people were poorly suited to the tasks assigned to them. As an example, budget control fell to a project manager who did not have the kind of detail-oriented mindset needed to work with numbers. He saw budget work as a chore and didn't pay close attention to the invoices that needed to be paid. In the previous construction project, the sizeable slush fund built into the budget was quickly consumed, which led to problems down the road. When a major supplier had trouble meeting its commitments, the company realized it would cost several extra million dollars to get the needed supplies on time. That led to extreme penny pinching (along the lines of, "Do you really need to use three nails in that spot or could you do with two?"). At one level, it sounds ridiculous that a project of this scope would reach that point, but we've seen similar disconnects in many, many contexts.

All told, the VPs cited countless examples of "poor communication." For one thing, communication was sporadic and reactive—people only sent emails or picked up the phone when a problem occurred. Think about that for a minute. If you've never been in a situation like this, just imagine what it's like to know that every single time you hear from someone it's because of a problem they think you caused. If you *have* been in that situation, you know the kind of resentment that builds up over time.

Secondly, the lines of communication were broken throughout and between the chains of command for all the groups. In some areas, the between-group communication was good but their hierarchical communication was poor (so the peers in different groups would talk to each other, but what one person told their boss would be different from what another person told a different boss). That led to duplication of effort and conflicting decisions made at different levels. There was also miscommunication associated with transitions and hand-offs from one group to the next.

Third, the groups didn't know the best ways to communicate with each other. For example, the engineers would prepare ultra-detailed, many-tabbed spreadsheets as status updates; the installation and manufacturing groups reading the update rarely got past page 1. Each of the groups was very defensive of its position, and much of the communication was actually emails or meetings where people were essentially saying, "Here's why I'm right and you're wrong."

As an aside, to make the communication problems even worse, the project management systems didn't talk to each other! The designers used one software system to track projects; the installation group used a completely different system. Updates from the designers might be sent to the installation group by a given deadline, but since it involved a great deal of manual effort to get the information fed into the other system, the installation group would have to begin its work before the systems were fully updated. The level of frustration was very high.

Had enough of the problems this company encountered? The list could go on, but by now you can probably recognize situations you've been in or witnessed in the past and know how far-reaching the effects of poor interaction can be! Each problem described here is something we see time and again when groups do not focus on interaction, and the more un-alike the groups are, the more they are separated by functional lines, the more likely that interaction problems will appear. That's one reason why silo issues are so common.

Perhaps it's not surprising that one of the biggest issues we helped the VPs recognize was that **they had done no interaction planning up front.** There was no discussion within or between the groups on how people could best work together, which led to many of the issues just discussed.

How do you break this cycle? The actions this company took were largely based on the ideas presented in this book. All key people experienced our decision-making simulation in conjunction with implementing new interaction development processes, including having their Team Roles analyzed. The groups all worked internally to develop clearer guidelines around roles, responsibilities, and decision-making authority. Key cross-functional groups also met and went through a mirror-imaging exercise to clear the air, after which they developed ground rules for their future interactions along with doing the same kind of work on roles and responsibilities that they had done within their groups. Most helpful was the alignment work done at the highest levels, between the VPs representing each functional group and the project leaders.

After this up-front work was completed, the groups began consciously dealing with interaction effectiveness as they worked on the next production line project, which, by way of a spoiler, they report was the easiest project they've ever run. The VPs told us that the new project went more smoothly than any previous project—despite the fact that the project manager was laid up in a hospital for several weeks as the result of a car accident.

They credit the speed and cordiality to changes such as:

- They used the Team Role analysis to help them make sure the right people were in the right jobs. They gained an understanding of the differences and importance of the many roles they had in play, which eased tension between the groups. This type of thinking is part of their standard operating procedures now.

- All the players used communication lines more often. People were in regular contact, so phone calls, emails, and texts were no longer *only* about problems. In fact, they were rarely so. More often, they were needed status updates or other useful proactive communications.

- They did more contingency planning. There was less need for panic reactions to problems because many likely issues were identified and plans put in place to deal with them. In addition, if something unexpected did occur, there was a standing guideline that the VPs would meet at the affected location within a day, discuss the issue together, and make an immediate call. This quick resolution by the top decision makers sped up the process and prevented countless problems down the line.

- Each VP visited the construction location twice a month—and on at least one of those days, they were all there at the same time.

Booster Shot

At some point, almost every company will launch a large initiative, perhaps forced on it by changes in laws (such as Sarbanes-Oxley), driven by a business priority (such as lowering operating costs or improving customer experiences), or as the consequence of other business decisions (such as mergers or reorganizations). What often happens with these initiatives is that the business leaders are clear about the business strategy—why the particular effort must be undertaken—and have a good handle on the operations (who, how, when). Nevertheless, they often fail to pay proper attention to the interaction aspect, which can lead to a wide range of problems.

For example, a major global company had a well-respected continuous improvement (CI) program that had produced good results. This company followed what has become the standard recipe for continuous improvement projects, sending a cadre of people through four weeks of training so they could became competent in problem solving, data collection and analysis, and project management. In addition, they went a step further than most CI programs: they also provided participants with a full week of training on some basic collaboration topics and methods.

The CI program was an enormous success for several years then lost some visibility and impact as the initial interest waned. One problem was that cycle times were too long, with many projects taking over a year to complete. Managers were not eager to invest their people or money resources in something that had such a long payback period.

When we examined this company's program, there was one obvious difference between how they treated the technical content and the interaction content *after* participants had completed the initial training. There were elaborate mechanisms in place to make sure that participants could apply their technical training on the job. For example, internal experts provided ongoing coaching and the company established an extensive knowledge base that was available online. After the initial course, participants met regularly in support groups so they could share challenges and ideas. There was no such post-training support for the interaction content. The company did a good job on the fun phase of interaction development but then abdicated responsibility for the mundane and tricky aspects of interaction, which meant that any gains from the one-week of training quickly faded away.

As a demonstration to prove that better interaction skills could boost the CI program's success and reduce project cycle time, we agreed to provide additional post-training interaction support to any project leaders who agreed to the following rules of the game:

- The trainees commit to a goal of a four-month cycle on their projects.

- Project teams will have a maximum number of six members (anything more than six becomes unwieldy in our experience).

- Every person on the trainees' teams (including the sponsor) undergoes the "fun" interaction development work so they understand their interaction strengths and weaknesses.

- Teams will map out their interaction strengths and weaknesses.

- The trainees will complete a simple checklist to monitor their team's interaction effectiveness (enforcing the mundane techniques).

- Trainees agree to form learning communities consisting of other trainees from their session and an expert guide (to help them deal with the tricky issues, among other things).

When these elements were added to the company's focus on reducing cycle time, the participants reported dramatic improvements. Here are some example comments:

Participant #1: Achieved a 5-month cycle time on a $500,000 project. "My team truly valued the personal insight gained from the interaction training and follow-up sessions. There was a stronger sense of commitment to the project because they got something for themselves out of participating. We were able to recognize team deficiencies that could impact our cycle time and discussed the risks they may pose to the project and how to mitigate them. These became part of our ground rules."

Participant #2: Achieved a 4-month cycle time. "The Team Mapping allowed team members who did not know each other to bond quicker and have awareness of the team behaviors each person brings."

Participant #3: Achieved a 6-month cycle time. "This project moved along well . . . which was not the case on my previous project. Having team members playing to their interaction strengths has been a huge help."

Cascading & Viral Models

If your company has a major initiative that an interaction program can be structured around, that is often a good starting point because people across the company will see the value that a focus on interaction can have. However, another effective way to introduce interaction into an organization is to start at any point where there is interest, passion, and energy, then work outwards from there. If that point of interest is the executive team, the effort then usually cascades down and out to the rest of the organization. If the starting point is any other kind of team, the best approach is to let its success spark interest in other areas and then follow up in those areas (the viral model). Here are examples of both of these approaches, plus one that combines the two:

Cascading deployment

An e-commerce startup in Silicon Valley ran into the kind of predictable problems that entrepreneurial businesses often encounter: A few years in, the two founders—one a visionary, the other a technical wizard—realized they were spending too much time bumping heads and not enough time growing the business. So they hired an experienced executive, Lloyd, to help them run and scale up the company.

What Lloyd discovered was a company deeply divided into silos. The product development people were hostile towards the technical group; the older warehouse employees working shift hours were frustrated by the "laid back" behaviors of the young, highly educated engineering staff who seemed to turn up for work whenever it suited them. This divisiveness was leading to problems as the company struggled to ramp up its fulfillment services, which had to handle over 22,000 SKUs.

Lloyd realized that neither the founder nor anyone else on the leadership team, let alone the rank and file, had paid any attention to the people issues that were dividing the company. An up-front survey and interviews revealed that many employees shared Lloyd's concerns in three interaction areas:

- Decision making and innovation
- Cross-functional collaboration
- Meeting effectiveness

These problems, in turn, created anxiety at the board level around execution of company strategies and the management of development projects.

To address these issues, Lloyd worked with the leadership team to develop a new strategic initiative they called "Design for speed and value," which had three goals:

1) An organizational design that would drive continuous process cycle time reduction.

2) A skilled, stable, and motivated workforce that would provide a competitive advantage in an industry with disproportionately high staff turnover rates.

3) Planning, interaction processes, and performance measurement systems that would create a culture of accountability and drive the attainment of organizational goals.

Lloyd first required the majority of employees to attend basic interaction training, and then began a more concentrated effort at the leadership level. The latter included working one-on-one with the two founders to address how they interacted with each other. Perhaps it will come as no surprise that the two founders had very different personalities and didn't really like each other all that much (and never would). But they realized they needed a way to work together effectively if their company was to survive. One key was to add more structure to their relationship around responsibilities and decision making. Previously, the visionary partner had created havoc by ordering people to work on her latest idea without regard to their previous commitments. That no longer happened.

Once Lloyd and the two founders were better aligned, the interaction work cascaded to the rest of the leadership team. Collectively, the company's leadership discovered they became much more effective both individually and as a team. Each leader then began to work with their own teams, and so on down the organization. The head of finance, for example, realized that his strengths were not in organizing his team or meeting preparation, but one of his direct reports was quite strong in those areas, so he delegated the bulk of those tasks to her.

After that top-down phase, Lloyd also had a facilitator do some silo-busting by conducting a number of cross-team sessions where representatives from the "warring parties" were able to work through sticky issues that had fueled the flames of rivalry. These sessions were productive in part because everyone had seen that their managers were also committed to improved interaction.

The various training sessions and follow-up work continued for the better part of 18 months, and the company saw more and more benefits as time went on. As just one example, originally, the website was a highly contentious issue. Working on interaction and collaboration helped all the people involved agree on a website design process and timeline—including deadlines after which no more changes could be made. The dynamics of the groups involved in designing and running the website completely shifted from resentful to trustful. The results were not only a much more robust customer experience, but also a lot less finger pointing internally.

In addition to seeing major changes in how the main tasks of the organization were handled—and much quicker decision making overall—the leaders reported noticing a much better morale.

Viral deployment

Unlike many of its competitors, a financial organization came out of the recent fiscal crisis relatively unscathed. However, the rapid changes in the business environment forced the company to undertake some serious self-examination, and the company's leadership team identified a number of major changes needed. One problem was the company's structure: the downturn in the economy revealed weaknesses and duplication in how it worked with its clients.

As a result of this analysis, the company undertook a major effort to centralize activities. That meant groups that used to operate independently now had to collaborate. Changing the structure of an organization with a very established culture of working in separate silos was a challenge.

One VP who was in charge of a major division realized that her staff needed help with collaboration. She was well respected in the company and had both positional authority and informal influence. When she wanted to get something done, she made sure it got done and was very accomplished at breaking down barriers. So she initiated a process to have her team of direct reports address their interaction issues. Here are the benefits she reported to us:

- People increased their ability to contribute effectively in team settings.

- Having a new language for discussing team behaviors and team effectiveness let the team deal with issues that previously had been un-discussable.

- Meeting times dropped by about 30% due in large part to better planning and preparation, including being consistent in defining what outcome was expected.

- There was significant improvement in the tactical skill set needed for improved team performance, which resulted in having fewer people involved in decision making, better documentation of decisions, speedier results, and greater buy-in to decisions.

The people who had been through the training then helped the VP establish a steering committee to oversee team effectiveness training and implementation in their division. That committee had four goals:

1) Keep continuous learning alive and model new behaviors

2) Monitor and measure the effectiveness of the training

3) Pursue corporate training and development support to improve effectiveness training based on what was learned in the pilot

4) Ensure this endeavor was a key component to achieving their strategic objectives

As these changes took hold, benefits began to accumulate rapidly. One team in this department reported "very favorable" results including higher productivity, which they credited to improved structures and logistics. This team became much more effective at drawing out minority views, which helped them routinely develop a broader set of options, which ultimately led to better decisions and buy-in.

The successes in this department and the division VP's support sparked interest in other areas of the company. The president of another division had a brand new management team that needed to solidify its decision-making ground rules and collaboration practices. He decided to use interaction methods as a mechanism to help that happen.

This pattern of sparked interest has continued. Today, several techniques (such as the 3Ps for meetings and norms around meeting management) are widespread throughout the company. In addition, other divisions have launched efforts to work on interaction. They have worked through the three steps described in the "home team" chapter (chap. 10) and are developing interaction plans to sustain the work.

Viral & cascading deployment

About a decade ago, a large U.S.-based manufacturing company began focusing on improving operations. One group began a very limited program around improving interaction as part of a larger process improvement initiative. As the word slowly got out that something different was happening with the people who had been through the interaction training, the head of operations asked the interaction trainer, "We don't really need to limit your interaction training to the process improvement work, right? Because there are a number of other areas in the company where it could really help us."

Soon after, this operations executive sponsored three interaction workshops that were open to people in any group, with special invitations issued to the VP of marketing and the VP of technology and development. Since the funding for the workshops was coming out of the operations budget, and because they were intrigued enough by this new idea, the VPs agreed to send people to the workshops. Overall, about 90 people attended the training over a three-month period, encompassing a wide range of attendees from up, down, and across the organization (including several senior executives and up-and-coming, high-potential directors and managers). This became a turning point for greater awareness of interaction issues and the adoption of collaborative techniques across different departments and divisions.

About 18 months in, a new senior executive was brought in to oversee both the operations group (led by the operations executive) and the supply chain operations. The new executive learned about the interaction efforts that had been going on in the operations group and was convinced by the results that this could improve relationships between the operations and supply chain groups and help in the establishment of an end-to-end culture.

From that point on, with the very active support of the human resources group and some strong internal interaction champions, there was a combination of viral pick-up and cascading efforts that had a broad positive impact on improving interaction. Every group gets the initial interaction training plus follow-up sessions that help them to continue building their skills.

There is a lot of lateral and vertical mobility in jobs within this company and people who have experienced great interaction in one job quickly recognize the interaction hotspots in their new jobs. (See sidebar, next page.) Consequently, there is an increasing demand for training and support.

The people in this company who have been practicing good interaction skills for several years are now applying them in multiple ways. For example, we mentioned their union negotiation team back in the chapter on conflict. Most of the negotiators on the company's side had been through interaction training, and they began applying what they had learned to the negotiation process, which included:

- Doing a check after each negotiating session on how well they had handled meeting management and interaction (such as rating how good a job they'd done at making sure everyone got to voice an idea).

- Creating a Team Map, the tool discussed in Chapter 4. That helped the negotiating team allocate tasks to the people best able to perform them.

The very seasoned lead negotiator credited their up-front interaction planning and the focus on interaction as one of the major contributors to the success of the negotiations.

Overall, there have been two fundamental shifts in this company that are leading to better dynamics and collaboration: first, more and more people are aware of the importance of the interaction piece (and can recognize interaction failures), and second, there is widespread knowledge about ways to improve interaction. People know that collaboration problems within a work group, between silos, or in a team don't have to be tolerated—they *can* be fixed.

Take Down the Hurdles

A leader we worked with recently said to us, "As we started to close our interaction gaps, we realized that we had shortened the distance from frustration to success—and that became quite a motivator for the team." That kind of motivation is critical because while it may be possible to force some kinds of change on an organization, different ways of interacting is not one of them. There has to be an incentive for people, groups, and organizations to put in the time and devote their energies to making better interaction a deliberate part of their lives.

When Effectiveness Becomes Infectious

Once you've experienced great interaction, you want to achieve that state with every group. The company has continued to invest in interaction, so it's become commonplace for the interaction experts to get calls from people that start out, "I went through the training a few years ago and it was great. Here are the problems in the group I work with now. . . . Do you think you can help?" "We have some people who just can't work together. What can we do?"

People get frustrated in environments with poor interaction. One executive, for example, reached out to us after changing jobs. "My new team isn't used to giving feedback," he said. "And we're just not aligned around how we're going to work together. They don't really know how to work with me, and vice versa."

One woman who took an executive position in a different company soon realized the enormity of the burden that poor interaction placed on her. "Meetings here are chaotic," she told us. "People don't know how to collaborate. They don't talk to each other about much of anything, let alone interaction issues. There's a lot of politics going on, which creates underutilized resources. Generally, the leaders aren't interested in or sensitive to interaction issues, which leads to silos like we used to have."

Fortunately, when it comes to interaction work, the benefits make the effort self-reinforcing: People gain immediate insights about their own talents and want to keep learning more. Leaders see they can get better results with less friction and greater commitment. Groups recognize they'd accepted norms that hindered their effectiveness and want to shape a better future. Organizations realize they can resolve (or at least move past) long-standing or critical stalemates that they'd come to accept as intractable.

Back in Chapter 1, we likened the effect of interaction gaps on an organization to hurdles on a running track. A hurdler can never go as fast as a sprinter on a flat track, and the more hurdles in your way, the slower you will go. The teams described in the previous chapter and the organizations featured in this chapter are becoming proactive in removing the hurdles that stand in the way of greater speed and effectiveness.

You will never be able to remove all the interaction hurdles in your organization, and new ones will always pop up, but how much faster and farther could you, your team, and your organization go if there were fewer and lower hurdles in your way and the ability to deal with them was fine-tuned?

Index

3

3Ps (purpose, process, preparation)
  definition of, 91
  examples of, 92–93

A

Alignment, 197
  and communication, 106–107
  misalignment, 100
  misalignment creep, 101
  staying aligned, 106
  tactical, 102

Allowable weakness. *See* Weaknesses, allowable

"And" not "but" rule, 113

B

Belbin, R. Meredith, 60

Burning platforms, 172

Burns, Robert, 109

C

Case Studies
  booster shot for CI program, 192
  cascading deployment in Silicon valley, 195
  cowboy & geek product development team, 1–3, 16–21
  dot problem, 39–40

James (new president who observes "craziness"), 23, 33
operations team implementation, 179
reduce project cycle time, 36–37
silo busting, 188
Solaris, 29–31
Solaris-done-right, 34
tech. mfg. executive team effectiveness, 37–38
technology development team, 181
viral & cascading deployment at mfg. co., 200–202
viral deployment at financial company, 198

Coherence (of interaction style), 156–169

Compliance without commitment, 27

Conflict, 25
  and trust, 130
  constructive
    example of, 129–130
    tips for, 132, 134
  destructive, example of, 127
  destructive vs. constructive, 125–130
  recover from blow-up, 138–140

D

Data sets (charts)
coherence scores, 157
executive time, 22
individuals not as smart as
teams, 14
Interaction gap, 13, 16
meeting airtime (participation),
85
meeting topics, outcomes, 80
predicting team success, 61

Death by silo, 25

Decision making, 27
exercise scenario, 12–14
"final decision maker" rule, 136

Defensiveness
characteristics of, 45, 114
difficulty in dealing with, 46–47,
113
in leaders, 162
lowering, 168

Dimensions of effectiveness,
3–4, 39

Disclosure
breaking the ice with, 121
definition, 119
examples of, 119

Discussion, dynamics of, 132

Dot problem, 39

Dunning, David, 59

E

Emotions, 44. *See also* Defensiveness

F

Fatal Flaws (implementation)
gravity of habit (underestimating norms), 48
head over heart (ignoring emotions), 44
one-and-done (training without
follow-up), 53
Tower of Babel (no shared
language), 47

Feedback, interaction, 109,
123
1-on-1, 118
barriers to, 111
group setting for, 115
guidelines for (in a group setting), 116–118
on group processes, 113

Ferrari in the garage, 54, 66,
67, 68, 155–169

Fun stuff, overview, 54

G

Ground rules, 135, 136, 178,
181

I

Interaction, description of, 4

Interaction, effective, 20, 35

Interaction Feedback. *See* Feedback, interaction

Interaction gap(s), 32
  defined, 4, 14
  impact of, 4, 5–6, 31

Interaction Plan, 176

Interaction problems, 24
  avoidance of participation, 28, 30
  compliance without commitment, 27
  conflict/culture clashes, 25
  stifled contributions, 28
  unexplained team failures, 26

Interaction quotient, 154

J

Johnson, Michael (sprinter), 11

M

Managing differences, 35

Meetings
  effectiveness, 37, 80, 82, 199, 201
  outcome orientation, 82–84
  participation data, 5
  participation, improving, 87–89
  size (recommendations for), 86

Mirror imaging activity, 17–18, 140–142

Mundane stuff, overview, 55

N

Norms (of a group)
  Creating new, 144–147, 171–186

definition of, 50
gravity of habit (difficulty in changing norms), 94
supportive vs. barrier, 51–52

P

Pain Points, 172

Purpose, of a team, 177, 180, 183

R

Risk planning, 184

Rutte, Martin, 49

S

Shared language
  benefits of, 65, 199
  failure to create (Tower of Babel), 47, 48

Strengths (Team Role)
  descriptions of, 63
  playing to, 67

T

Team Maps
  description of, 71
  examples of, 72
  interpreting and using, 72–74, 74, 180, 183

Team Roles
  adapting to gaps or overlaps, 73–74, 76
  model, 60
  role definitions, 63

Team Roles, cont.
  using to improve effectiveness,
    134, 135, 144, 155, 158, 163,
    177–186

Track race (sprinter vs. hurdler),
  11

Tricky stuff, overview, 56

U

Un-discussables, 114, 121, 199

V

Versatility
  individual, 70
  leader, 163

W

Weaknesses, allowable
  examples by Team Role, 63
  managing, 68, 158–160

WIIFM (what's in it for me?),
  103–104, 123

WIIFU (what's in it for us?),
  103, 104

Y

Young, Kevin (hurdler), 11

Reminder!

All of the resources referenced in this book can be found at:

www2.3circlepartners.com/interaction-gap-resources

On this site, you'll find links to:

- An annotated Team Role report, a sample report showing how the data on one person's collaborative strengths and weaknesses should be interpreted

- An example of a Team Map, which shows all of the Team Role strengths and gaps on one team and how that information is helpful

- The Interaction Index, a tool for helping groups evaluate and monitor their interaction effectiveness

You will also find other FREE resources, including articles on team effectiveness.

80194840R00124

Made in the USA
San Bernardino, CA
24 June 2018